Art Now Cornwall

Contents

St IVES
TATE

Published by Tate St Ives
Supported by Tate St Ives Members
Edition 2,000

Introduction

Susan Daniel-McElroy and Sara Hughes

This is the first exhibition presented by Tate St Ives which includes a curatorial selection of works by a significant number of artists living and working in Cornwall. *Art Now Cornwall* is not a survey of artists working in Cornwall but an exciting opportunity to sample current practice across a wide range of media. The scope of the exhibition includes twenty-eight artists spanning three generations, with the oldest artist aged sixty and the youngest aged thirty. (From our perspective, an understanding of contemporary practice across a span of thirty years is relevant to determining new themes in artists' work.)

This important exhibition was initiated to meet popular demand by artists and audiences following the public consultation process informing the gallery's expansion plans in 2005. It is also an opportunity for the public to appreciate the emerging opportunities that exist for artists in Cornwall through Tate St Ives' Residency Programme, Education and Exhibition Programme and the many cultural agencies and opportunities that have been established in the past five years.

When we began our research, the overall aim was to learn as much as possible about practice in Cornwall and to build fruitful relationships with the artists we met. Due to limitations on our time, funding and gallery space, this exhibition is only a starting point for what we hope may have a legacy and be repeated in future years, either by Tate St Ives in its expanded state or other institutions in Cornwall such as the Exchange and Newlyn Gallery. The exhibition, publication and education programme aims to present and discuss the major themes that are emerging from artists' practice in the region and how they relate to the wider context of contemporary practice in the UK.

Art Now Cornwall includes forty-nine works made by twenty-eight artists who live and work mainly in West Cornwall. In the course of researching this exhibition, we looked at more than forty artists' work and made thirty-five studio visits based on existing knowledge and recommendations from colleagues in other contexts. We embarked upon an engaging journey of discovery to find a rich diversity of practice that has built an impressive exhibition which includes painting, photography, print-making, sculpture, live art, drawing and video. With only very few exceptions, selections were made from works recently made or found in the studio and in that sense, the selection is an honest sampling of current contemporary practice. We have chosen works on the basis of tailoring them to the particular architecture of the gallery, how they will relate to one another and the ensuing dialogues which occur between them.

Subjects and themes in *Art Now Cornwall* obviously reflect the focus and interests of the artists, some of which are more private and introspective than others. Some trajectories that run through the exhibition link to various artistic strategies such as Surrealism, appropriation, formalism, interpretation, nostalgia, childhood memories, play and narration, amongst others. These subjects reveal the contemporary concerns of artists in our locale and it is interesting to contemplate how these relate to a wider sense of contemporary art practice.

Given the legacy of late English Modernism in St Ives for example, we were surprised not to find some critiquing of past practice such as formalism, or the deconstruction and reinterpretation of Modernism's coda. However, we were also surprised to find that the landscape is not a predominant subject for many artists. Cornwall is particularly rich in strong painting and this is interesting to note in a year where the Turner prize has been won by the female painter Tomma Abts. Cornwall has relatively few sculptors, possibly reflecting the paucity of foundries, workshops and residency opportunities for sculptors.

What else have we discovered in the course of making this exhibition? We have been struck by the determination, despite the isolation, of many artists often working in remote coastal communities. Contrast their reality, for example, with those artists based in urban contexts where they would have accessible resources such as affordable transport, a library, art materials, technical support and workshops. Artists also need to see quality exhibitions showing new models of practice and be with their peers enjoying other aspects of popular culture such as film and new media. In this instance, the mixed programming of contemporary art alongside historical displays of Modernist and other works from Tate's Collection, become even more significant as an artists' resource.

Nevertheless, Cornwall is an exciting place for artists to be developing their practice now. And there is hope for a new generation of Fine Art graduates to gain confidence to stay in Cornwall with the development of the Combined Universities of Cornwall and, in particular, University College Falmouth's and Cornwall College's new courses that include business skills.

The creation of many studio spaces in the old Grammar School in Redruth, the renovation of studios at Porthmeor in St Ives and Trewarveneth in Newlyn will further help artists' development and networks. Since the establishment of Tate St Ives Artist Residency Programme in early 2003, a number of other residency opportunities have already developed in partnerships between the independent and commercial sectors. The development of the St Ives Painting School, St Ives Archive & Study Centre, the Leach Pottery and Tate St Ives Phase 2, will also provide employment opportunities for artists either working in new residencies or with innovative education programmes.

Since Tate St Ives opened in 1993, there are now more than sixty commercial galleries in St Ives alone and – in anticipation of developments at The Exchange and possibly, the Royal Cornwall Museum – growing numbers in Penzance and Truro. Clearly, with the development of Arts Council South West's *Art Cred* scheme, allowing collectors to buy interest free over several months, Cornwall is a vibrant commercial context for artists to sell their work. More importantly, there are an increasing number of affluent and confident collectors investing and building their collections with significant works by emerging artists.

There is also a growing cultural infrastructure and more opportunities available with the establishment of several creative agencies such as Creative Skills, Cornwall Arts Marketing and the Creative Unit thanks to Cornwall Arts Trust and Objective 1 funding. Creative Partnerships and Projectbase Cornwall are supported through a strategy for visual art developed by the Arts Council of England South West as is the creation of The Exchange and the improved Newlyn Gallery facilities. Projectbase (previously St Ives International), will initiate external projects with international artists, further developing new opportunities for artists in our locale.

Some of these agencies are at an early stage in their development and still evolving but all of them will contribute to a young artist's confidence to find a way of working in Cornwall and be part of the critical debate surrounding new models of practice. It cannot be said too many times that what is so vital to artists of any age is the accessibility of seeing other artists' work of the highest standard in exhibitions and some financial support to allow the possibility of national and international travel. Without being able to regularly see important exhibitions in London or presentations at the Venice Biennale (every two years) and Documenta (every five years), for example, how can an artist living in Cornwall assess their practice and take confidence in their ideas in relation to what is going on elsewhere? Without being able to infiltrate social and professional networks with their peers in London and elsewhere in the world, how can they begin to show their work in an international context? With Convergence funding coming on stream in 2007 and Cornwall bidding to Europe as a Region of Culture in 2012, it is even more vital that investment is made into all aspects of artists' practice in good time for that celebratory moment to come when Cornwall managed to rewrite the rules that apply to Capital of Culture.

Amanda Lorens

Amanda Lorens works in the space between particular social situations and live art. Incorporating video and audio installation with live art, her current work uses Tango to reveal the intimacy of human inter-relationships. Lorens has tapped into a popular cultural zeitgeist with her new work *Tango Privado* 2007. Across the nation, as a result of programmes like *Strictly Come Dancing*, dance classes – particularly in Latin American dance – are springing up. On the high street, the fashion industry has been influenced by the style of dress which accompanies these exciting dances. But it is important to note that Lorens is fascinated by the subtle complexities of Argentine Tango which is not as 'showy' as conventional ballroom Tango.

Tango Privado exists in two parts. Both the live art installation and the video *Tango Privado II* 2007, are developed from *Tango In-Transit*, 2006, performed in the back of a Luton van on Penzance sea front in August. Lorens turns viewer to voyeur in a kind of Tango peep show with monologues selected from replies to an email questionnaire sent to Tango dancers in 2006. Dancers were asked to confide their private and most intimate experiences of Tango. By displaying tango in an obscured and confined space, the artist uses the dance to explore notions of human relationships and boundaries in relation to obsession, intimacy, conflict, desire and sensuality.

Lorens was a founder member of Penwith Artist Led Projects or PALP, where she co-curated context-specific exhibitions in temporary and unusual locations, such as the Telephone Exchange in Penzance – due to become the Exchange Gallery on completion in 2007. She has exhibited nationally and internationally and has been engaged in international research in India, Australia, Italy, Albania and South America. Much of her recent work is inspired by these travels, from filming laundry being washed on the banks of the River Ganges to tango in the atmospheric dance halls of Buenos Aries.

Tango Privado appears to highlight the paradox between identity and uniformity in the power and vulnerability of each individual as they carry out the most intimate of movements in this complex dance. It is this paradox that she seeks to make visible by concentrating the viewer's attention on intimate information, poses, attitudes, gestures and gazes prevalent in those individuals who dance the Tango.

Selected Biography

1969
Born Gibraltar

1997–8
MA Fine Art,
Chelsea College of Art, London

1987–90
BA (Hons) Fine Art,
Winchester School of Art

Selected Exhibitions and Residencies

2006
Outsider Artist's video, Princess Pavilion, Falmouth

Tango In Transit live art, audio installation. In Transit Mobile Art Projects, Part of Tract live Art, co-curated by Newlyn Art Gallery and Art Surgery

2005
Landings Trebah Gardens, Cornwall, site related audio installation.

Awning project, artist's video, Bristol

2004
Vertigo collaborative multi media, live art installation, Newlyn Art Gallery, Newlyn

2003
Transitions Mahalaxmi Dhobi Ghat, Video, Audio, live art installation, Newlyn Art Gallery, Newlyn

Wish You Were Here touring exhibition of art works in suitcases, (PALP)

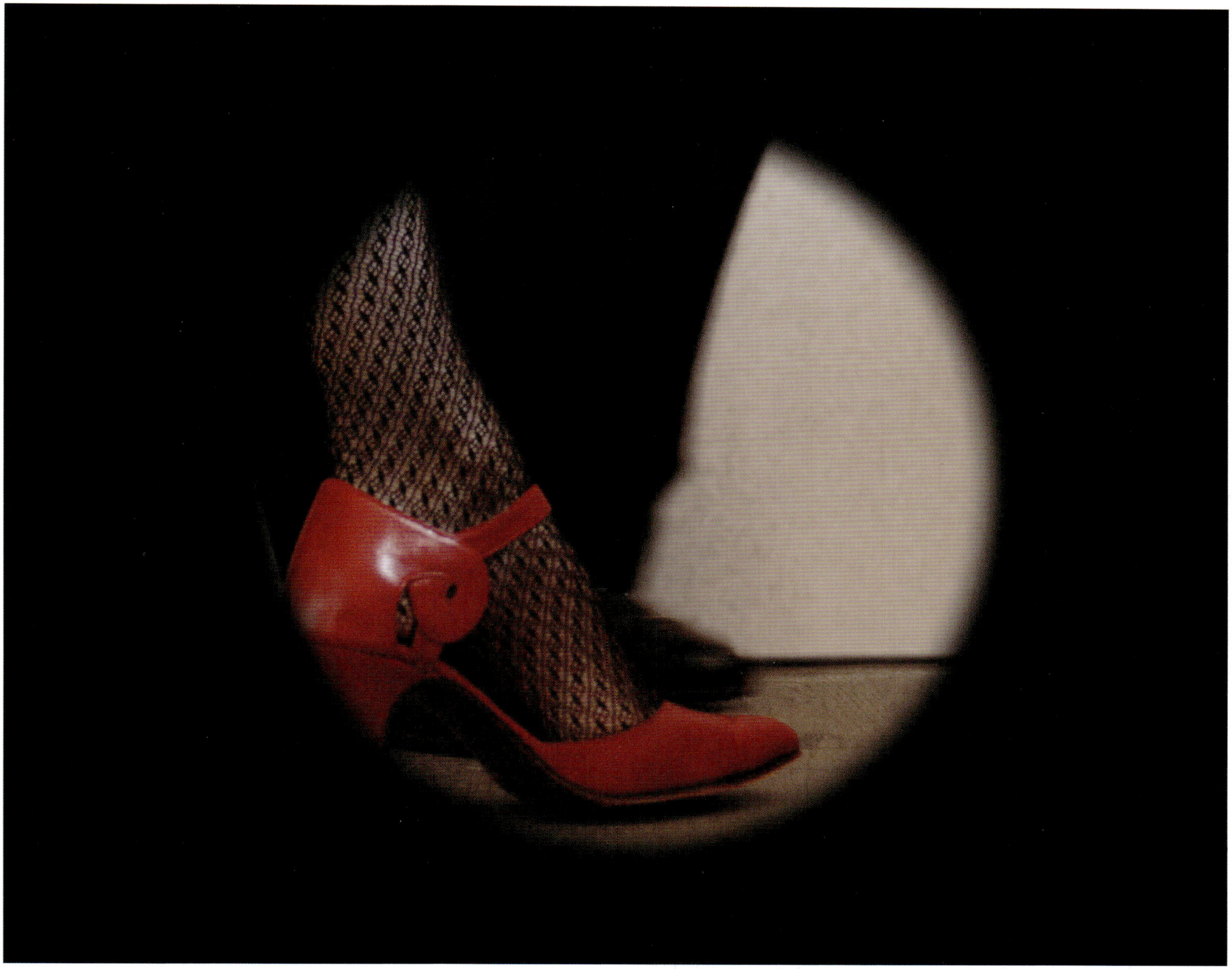

Tango Privado 2007, Photograph © the Artist

Andy Currie

The makeshift and dexterous improvisation of materials we would not normally associate with art belies this artist's skill in animating the everyday, to touch our imagination and give pleasure in his tricks for the eye. *My Lucky Star is a Rubbish Scorpion* 2004, is a mere strip of black plastic which dances randomly in a breeze generated by one fan recycled from a computer hard drive. This animated scrap momentarily poses in the form of said creature about once a minute, causing fascination for viewers of any age and highlights the lyrical possibilities in the most banal circumstances, if we have the wit to spot it.

Currie is adept at choosing his materials in relation to the compatibility of their purpose in his finished low-tech kinetic sculptures – which often have an affinity with the irreverent and experimental works of the Swiss artists Peter Fischli and David Weiss. In *Blustery Showers* 2004, for example, the combination of rippling black plastic and air generated by two household fans really does sound like a shower of rain. The two fans face each other, with a large square of black plastic in between. The plastic is self-suspended and becomes fixed between two opposing air flows, causing the material to ripple and create abstract forms at high speed. In *Egg and Spoon Race* 2006, the futility of human endeavour seems to be referenced as a plastic cup captures a ping pong ball under the influence of a mechanically contrived wind.

Gylling Dune 2006, recreates the myth of how sand dunes are created in a simulation of the wind's action in a tiny confined environment. The combination of breeze and sand create a perfect spiral that is perpetually in motion, forming and reforming endlessly in a Zen-like action. The ability to harness the poetic and potentially mediocre through the banality of poor materials is a magician's transformative gesture – rare amongst artists.

Selected Biography

1977
Born Dollgellau, Wales

1996
Diploma in Art Foundation Studies,
West Suffolk College

1999
BA Fine Art,
Falmouth College of Art

2005
PGCE (pcet),
Cornwall College

Solo Exhibitions

2004
Zero Gallery, Berlin
340 Old Street, London

2003
340 Old Street, London

2002
Cairns Regional Gallery, Australia

2000
The Raw Gallery, London

Selected Group Exhibitions

2007
Some Vacant Accomodation Stroud Valley Artspace, Gloucestershire

2006
X15: A programme of artists' film and video, screening as part of *The Emma Hart Biennale* Ada Street Gallery, London
250 Ouvres petis formats, Galerie Chybulski, France
EEK The Old Redruth Grammer School, Cornwall

2005
Inverse Newlyn Art Gallery, Newlyn
British Art Salon der Erste Stock, Berlin

2004
Seller Konigstadt Brauerei, Berlin

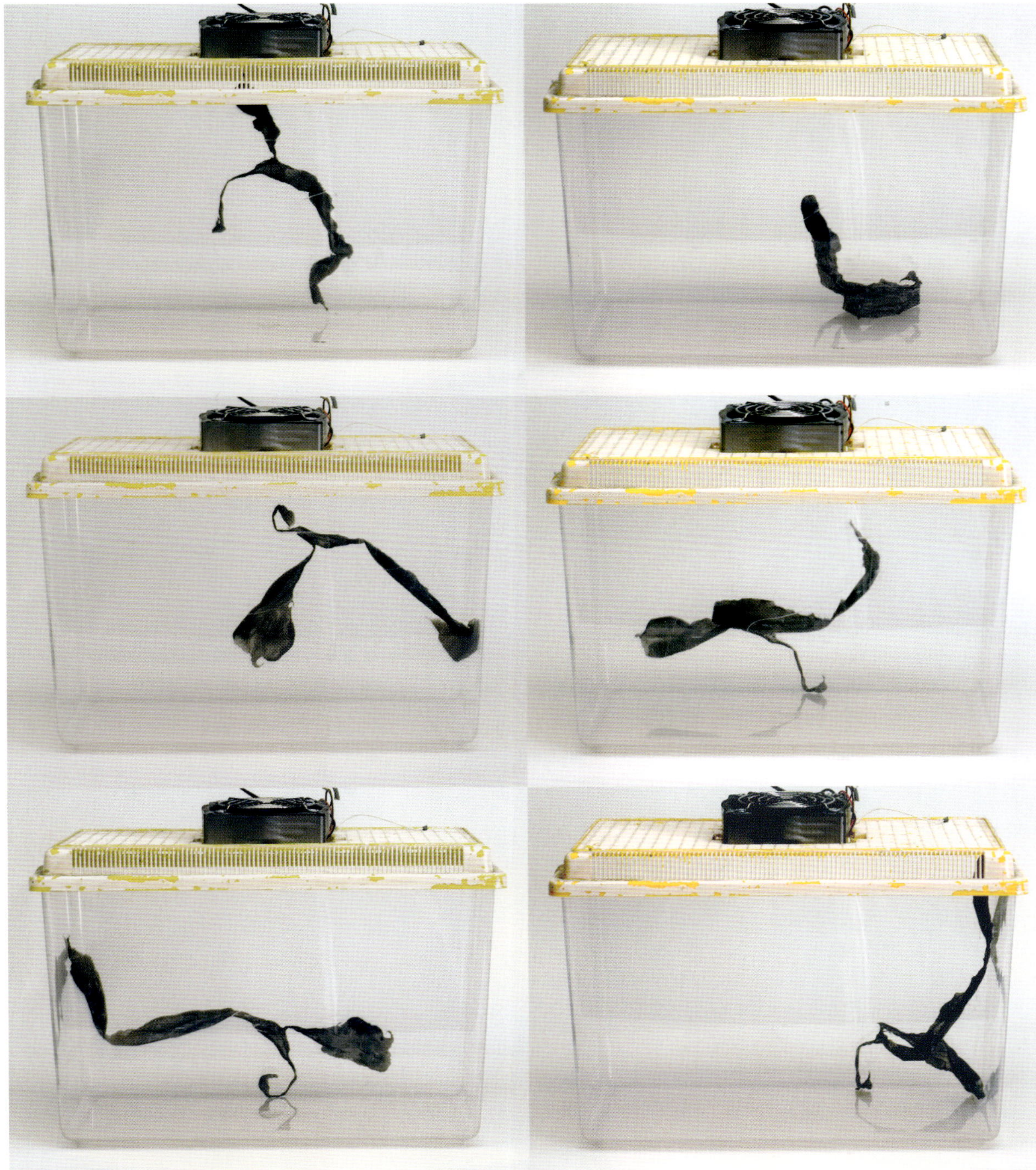

My Lucky Star is a rubbish Scorpion 2004, Mixed media, 23 x 35 x 23 cm © the Artist

Andy Hughes

The images in this exhibition come from *Dominant Wave Theory*, a recently published book of photographs made on various beaches around West Cornwall, Scotland and the USA over the last six years. An active member of Surfers Against Sewage, his photographs consider the epic and the everyday in the detritus washed up on the region's shorelines. These are not ordinary photographs but express the latest twenty-first century developments in mass market colour photography – plastic on plastic you might say.

In terms of subject matter and approach, some of these images recall the work of Keith Arnatt and his exhibition *Rubbish and Recollections* 1989. Originally a conceptual sculptor in the 1970s, Arnatt placed his photographic work firmly in the British Landscape tradition with his *Polythene Palmers* 1987, photographs which ironically depicted Arcadia as described by Samuel Palmer in his utopian visions of landscape.

Whilst Hughes' images of plastic depicted in heroic scale may give us some concern about waste material and its impact on a sensitive maritime environment, there is another side to these intelligent images. Hughes presents us with not only an ecological message but a knowing and heady rush through artistic strategies using the power of photography's saturated colour to highlight, frame, and play with scale, in an irreverent awareness of art historical practices.

Using technical aspects of the medium to portray a tiny object as something of heroic scale is a favourite trick of photography as is the careful crop and use of the rectangle to suggest something beyond the picture plane (for example, an extensive landscape). In the context of the St Ives School, the artist's knowledge has influenced a number of these images. But it is the distinctive nature of the medium that has been exploited all too often; photography has the capacity to picture the world in a most mysterious manner. It is as if the technology had a direct connection with the artist's Id, where the collective experiences of his physical and cultural landscape that have soaked into his mind reside.

Perhaps this is why some of the objects portrayed here remind us of other things, suggesting a transformation has been made by the processes that govern photography. Why is it that a shard of plastic looks like a crashed UFO? How can it be that a piece of foam looks a bit like Robbie the Robot circa 1951 or a monster (depending on which way you look at it)? And how stunning is that landscape which has the look of granite and stitching at the same time as it shocks you into realising that it is really the chain-mail gloved hand of a resting Saracen Knight?

Selected Biography

1966
Born Castleford, West Yorkshire

1985–9
BA (Hons) Fine Art,
University of Wales Institute – Cardiff

1989–91
MA Fine Art Photography,
Royal College of Art, London

**Recent Grants,
Fellowships and Awards**

2006
Arts Council England

2003, 2004
Shortlisted Artist, British Antarctic Survey
(shortlisted consecutively)

2000
National Lottery and Millennium
Commission Award

Selected Exhibitions

2006
Core Gallery, The Eden Project, Cornwall
Invited selected artist *Danger Global Warming* Blacksmoke and Greenpeace

2004–5
Oxbow Longboard Art Project, various
galleries across the UK

Collections

Cornwall County Council; Arts Council
in Wales; Private collections

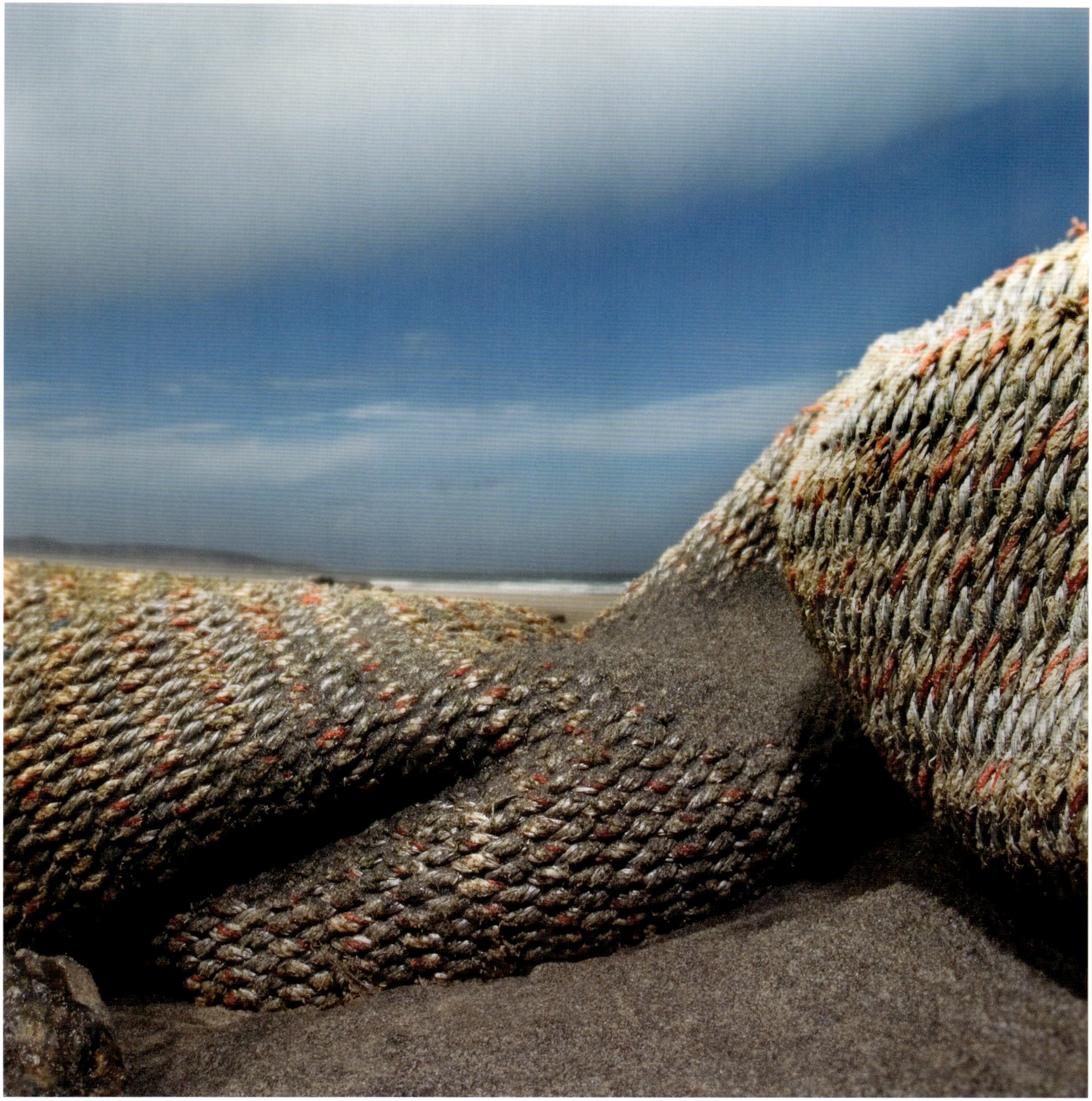

Gwithian Beach 2005, Photograph, 51 x 51 cm © the Artist

Jonty Lees

The creativity of child play and childhood memories of gadgets and games are at the heart of Jonty Lees' practice. In 2003, he constructed a spectacular version of a velodrome for Newlyn Gallery's Transition series of exhibitions for emerging artists. Actively engaging the viewers as participants in the making of this kinetic work, the wooden banked cycle track presented a robust physical challenge to all who attempted to ride it. Although it was relatively straightforward to circle the track to the top level, it was infinitely more difficult to reach the safety of the floor again and many participants fell at the moment of this realisation.

In this more recent work *Skimming Stones* 2005, a clay pigeon trap or shooting machine was modified by the artist to regularly throw out adjusted clays (upside down and smoothed off) which skim the surface of a lake. By making this small adjustment (after all, all art is just a small adjustment), Lees has liberated the machine from a context of sport and violence into a time-wasting and daydreaming context. In a way, you might say that the object has been transformed from a perfectly useful machine to a relatively useless machine.

When skimming stones without the support of a mechanical device, it is usual to spend hours looking for flat stones, attempting to throw the stone properly in order to ensure it skims well, observing its flight and achieving at least three bounces (this is the preferred objective). Using the machine, however, allows the participants to concentrate exclusively on the joyous moment when the stone skims the water, rather than focussing on the aspects of perfecting technique or any competitive spirit between participants.

Lees' unpretentious production methods incorporate poetic moments in their realisation and gravity appears to be a recurring theme in his work. To accompany the video of *Skimming Stones*, the artist commissioned Andrew Palmer to make a romantic representation of a stone skimming the surface of water. This idea came to him on appreciating how the renowned Scottish artist Ian Hamilton Finlay worked with other artists to realise many different types of objects of both modest and classic beauty. The work in its final state now includes a video representation of the action of the machine shown alongside the painting of the final aspect of the action, making a neat circular reference to representation in two contexts; the *cinema-verite* of the film and video which always attracts our attention because it seems 'real' to us and the romantic artifice that is the painting. Despite its accepted artifice the painting recalls the nostalgia of the moment rather than the banality of the mechanical act which strips the task of its reward.

Selected Biography

1971
Born Bangor, North Wales

2000–3
Falmouth College of Art

2003–5
Slade School of Art

Selected Group Exhibitions

2007
Some Vacant Accomodation Stroud Valley Artspace, Gloucestershire

2006
Moot Gallery, Nottingham
The Emma Hart Biennale Ada Street Gallery, London

2005
Somewhere in-between Galleri KIT, Trondheim Academy of Fine Art
Video London1 Barcelona, Spain

2004
Sounding Out Festival University East London

2003
Transitions 3 Newlyn Art Gallery, Newlyn

Awards

AHRC Professional Preparation Master's Scheme

Collections

Ernst and Young

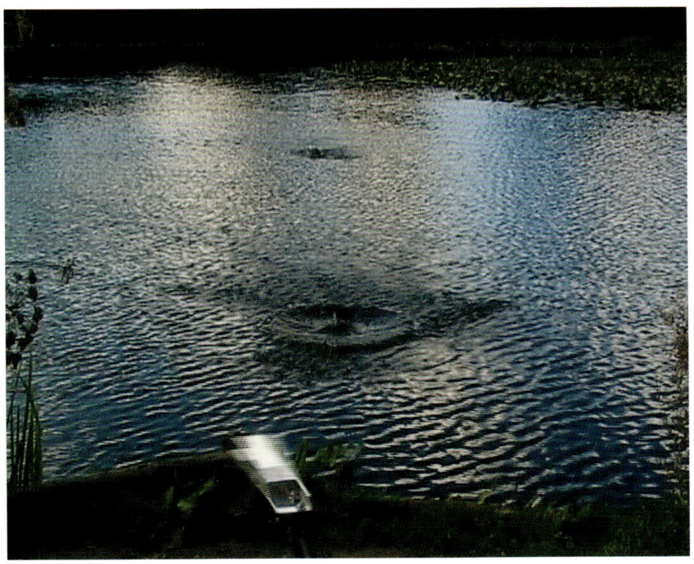

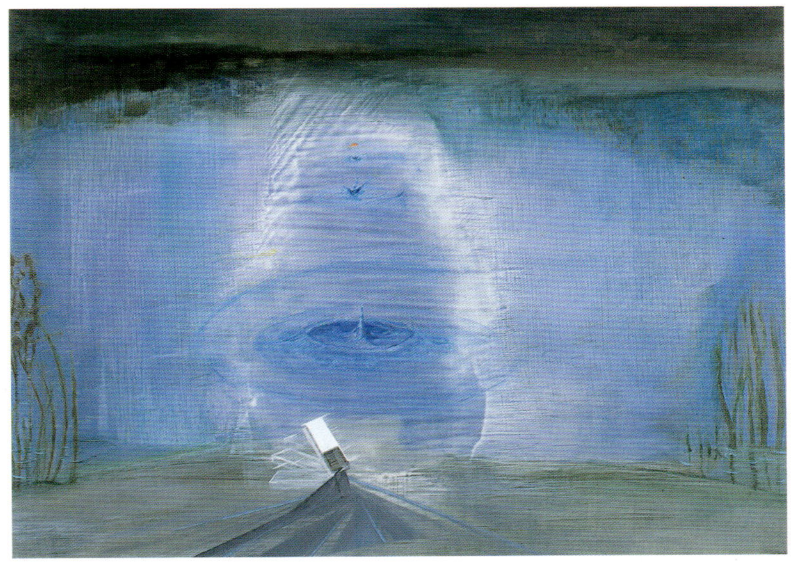

Skimming Stones 2005, Video © the Artist

Skimming Stones 2005, Oil on Linen, 41 x 59 cm © the Artist, Painting by Andrew Palmer

Matthew Lanyon

The paintings of Matthew Lanyon – on first glance – inescapably recall the later paintings of his father Peter Lanyon. But Matthew Lanyon is evolving his own language of forms, working his way through ideas, sorting out his thoughts about what painting is, what it can be and where he is taking it in the difficult context of following his father's footsteps.

A self-taught artist, he bears the trademarks of a natural painter who continues to evolve. He has as much rigour and self-doubt as any artist who has been trained – perhaps even more than those who have formally studied how to be articulate about their work. In the last five years he has made two hundred and fifty paintings – mainly for a commercial context – and success has raised his game to make paintings of scale that may reach, eventually, beyond the commercial gallery context.

He is interested in information gathering and the process of its assimilation. His paintings are a synthesis of living and remembered experiences, including contact with other people and observations of natural systems such as the movement of constellations and how these can be measured and retold.

The recent painting *Highground III* was painted in 2006 and here is the artist's description of it. "The painting comes from a trip to Lomnica in the Tatra mountains in Slovakia in May 2004. Three thousand feet above the town is a glacial lake and an observatory. A cable-car rises a further 3,000 feet to the summit on a twenty minute white-knuckle eternity of slow-moving vertical rock-face and vertigo. In the painting, points of the compass are brought back in. From North, for all the hay in Poland. South, over the plains of Hungary, the Ukraine. East was a concrete 'CCCP' and a symbol of the heavens over the observatory doorway and West, for all those carved madonnas and our guide, who took us over the mountain on crutches."

Selected Biography

1951
Born St Ives, Cornwall

1969–73
BA (Hons) Combined Sciences, Leicester University

Selected Solo Exhibitions

2003–6
Rainyday Gallery, Penzance
Minster Fine Art, York

Selected Group Exhibitions

2005
Wiseman Originals, London
New Grafton Gallery
The John Davies Gallery

2004
The John Davies Gallery, Stow-on-the-Wold
Wiseman Originals, London
The Hutson Gallery, London
Platform 100 Exhibition, London

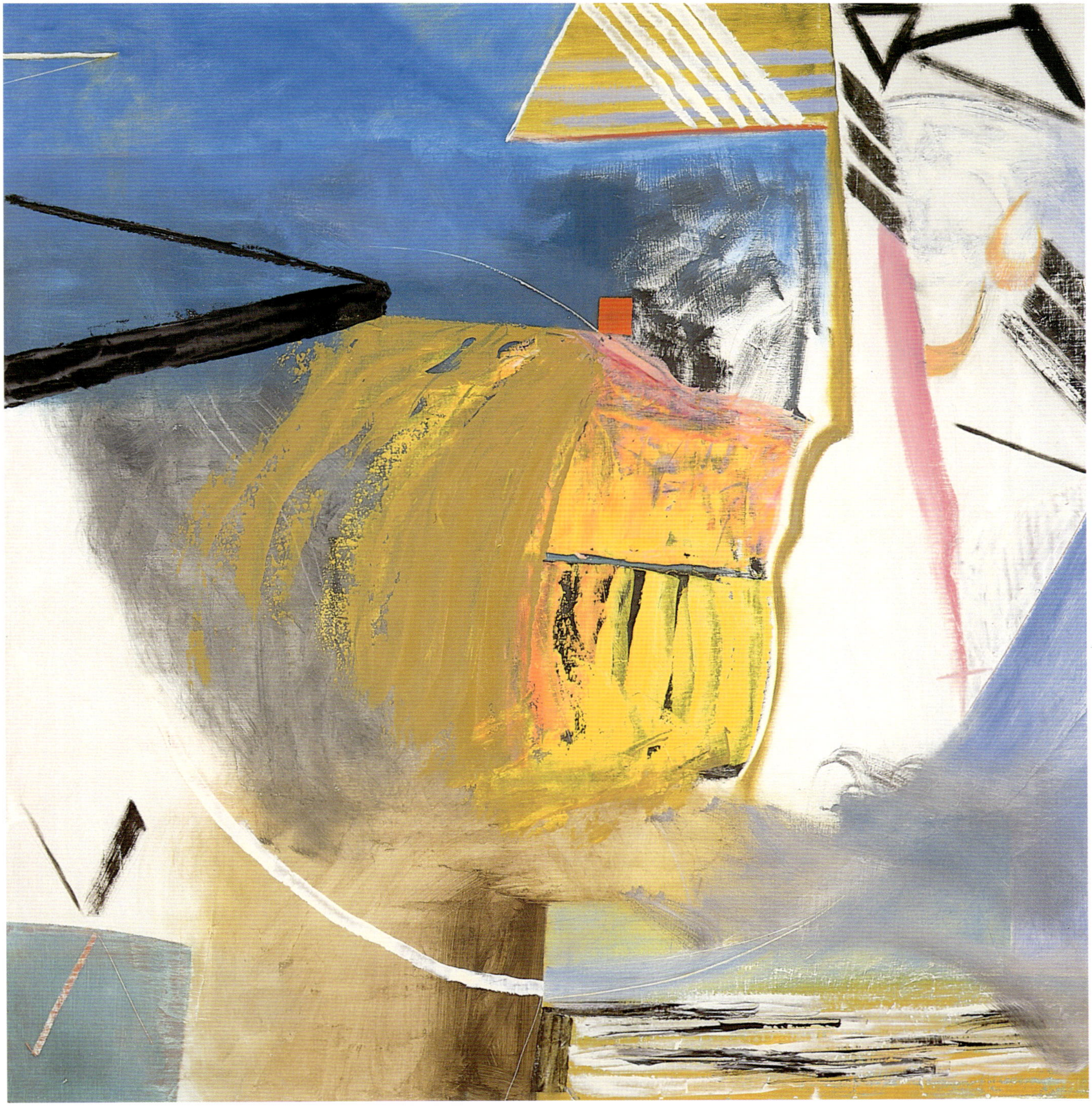

Highground III 2006, Oil on canvas, 168.9 x 168.9 cm © the Artist

Michael Porter

How can a painter reinvest the basic tenets of modernist painting with a spark of life? Today, painting is almost inconceivable for many artists without the photograph. Recalling photorealist paintings of the 1960s, photography can condition the way we see painting; even more so nowadays, it changes the way painting is made. Making paintings that express something of the language of photography is now a familiar strategy for artists. It is a given that artists set out to avoid the elephant trap of photographic verisimilitude, which can have a dampening or redundant effect on the viewer. There are two ways that photographic vision enters Porter's paintings. The first might be the way that the camera portrays everything within the frame in similar focus (a feat that the human eye cannot achieve). The second is the objective distancing that the camera always achieves and which has the effect of an alienation of the image or a removal of the 'real'. A classic example of this effect would be the photographs of James Fenton portraying the horror of the Crimean War in shocking images of dead soldiers which the camera – with its distancing lens – has managed to make beautiful.

Issel Road 2006, was inspired by a particular situation in a rural context. Driving down a country lane outside the village of Issel, Porter could see on a grassy verge, what seemed to be several eggs, crisp and shiny, standing out very distinctly from their surroundings. On closer inspection the objects turned out to be a profusion of wild apples scattered alongside the lane in a most incongruous configuration. Some were half hidden amongst their surroundings and others, lay, as if placed, on the surface of the grass, like eggs in a nest. The artist recorded this strange incidence with his camera in the hope that it would prove useful as an aide memoire for a future studio painting.

Cornish Stones 2006, were conceived as a result of walking along the beach at Newlyn, collecting stones and discovering them again in his pocket several days later. In some instances stones were placed directly onto photographic paper and subsequently exposed to light. Others were produced by painting on a plastic sheet in order to make a handmade negative from which a photographic print was made. These photographic bases are reworked with various paints as a way of recreating the character and atmosphere of the sea. Whilst stones are the subject of the work they also play a large part in their actual making and, as such, the means of making becomes the subject, where the natural object is used to describe nature.

Selected Biography

1948
Born Holbrook, Derbyshire

Solo Exhibitions

2007
Jane Deering Fine Art, Boston, USA
Going to ground Purdy/Hicks Gallery, London

2005
Works on Paper Purdy/Hicks Gallery, London

2004
Shell, sitting still Cape Ann Historical Museum, Gloucester, Massachusetts
Mantserrat College of Art Gallery, Beverly, Massachusetts
Scanning the Ground Purdy/Hicks Gallery, London

2003
Works on Paper Purdy/Hicks Gallery, London
Pathless Woods and Lonely Shore Derby Museum and Art Gallery

Selected Collections

Arts Council; British Council; British Museum (Alexander Walker Bequest); Contemporary Arts Society; Contemporary Art Museum, Warsaw, Poland; Government Art Collection; National Gallery, London; Royal Botanic Gardens, Kew; Royal West of England Academy, Bristol; Birmingham Museum and Art Gallery; Harewood House; Bolton Art Museum; Leicestershire Education Authority; Smolyan Art Gallery, Bulgaria; Sunderland Museum and Art Gallery; University of Nottingham; University of Warwick; Museum of the Natural World; National Gallery of Australia, Canberra; Deutsche Bank; New York Public Library; Unilever; Arthur Andersen and Co; Whitworth Art Gallery, University of Manchester; National Gallery of South Africa, Cape Town

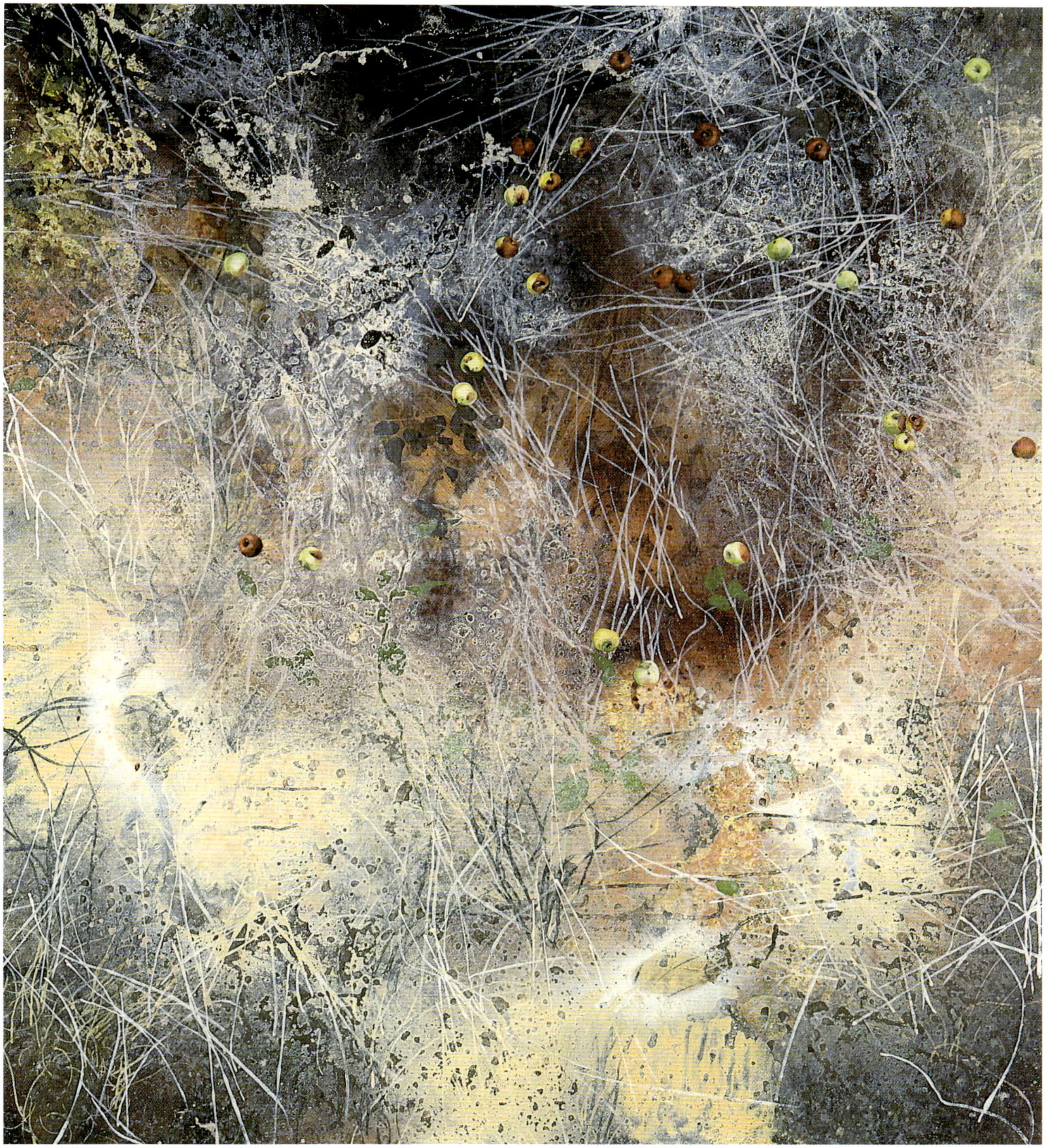

Issel Road 2005, Acrylic and oil on canvas, 121 x 111 cm, Purdy Hicks Gallery, London © the Artist

Andy Whall

Andy Whall is a founder of *Art Surgery* an organisation which initiates artists' projects, often with collaborating organisations, to be presented in locations beyond the gallery walls. His current practice is performance-based with drawing and time-based media – mainly video – used as an accompaniment. Often the performance is action-based; for example, in a recent work, he was blindfolded and whilst kneeling, licked a granite pillar for four hours. The use of the blindfold was to enhance his sense of vulnerability whilst carrying out a ritualistic sequence of actions in a Cornish landscape setting which had previously been mined.

His works are often about the mind and body's physical propensity for endurance under extreme conditions, such as running continuously or climbing (or licking). He sees the shoreline not as a picturesque subject but as a contentious point of exchange between humanity and the natural world. His practice is about engagement with the landscape in an unexpected fashion, addressing how we perceive it in relation to the physical activities which take place either at the ocean's edge or within the landscape, such as surfing and climbing across rock faces at the edge of the ocean. In a recent video work he became interested in the zone between high and low tide, intrigued by the idea of using time-based media to frame a section of landscape we would not be able to register under normal conditions.

The work in this exhibition *In An Atlantic Wave* 2006, has been filmed underwater by the artist and takes our imagination away from the literal manifestation of the landscape and into a phenomenological engagement with stone and water. Because of the manner in which the video has been made, we take the place of the artist and experience the depths of the ocean, first moving into darkness and then moving up towards the surface of the sea.

Selected Biography

1964
Born Cardiff

1983–6
BA (Hons) Fine Art,
University of Wales Institute, Cardiff

1987–9
MA Fine Art,
University of Wales Institute, Cardiff

Selected Performances, Installations and Exhibitions

2007
New St Ives School 1997–2007, UWIC

2006
Wheal Art Weekend, Art Place and History
Site-ations, International, Europe, Sligo

2005
60 seconds video work group show, Penzance

2004
Traverse. Ignite. Acorn Theatre, Penzance

2002
Cluster Mixed media Show, Dublin

Awards

2005
ACESW Seminar grant

2004
ACSW Research grant

2003
ACESW seminar grant

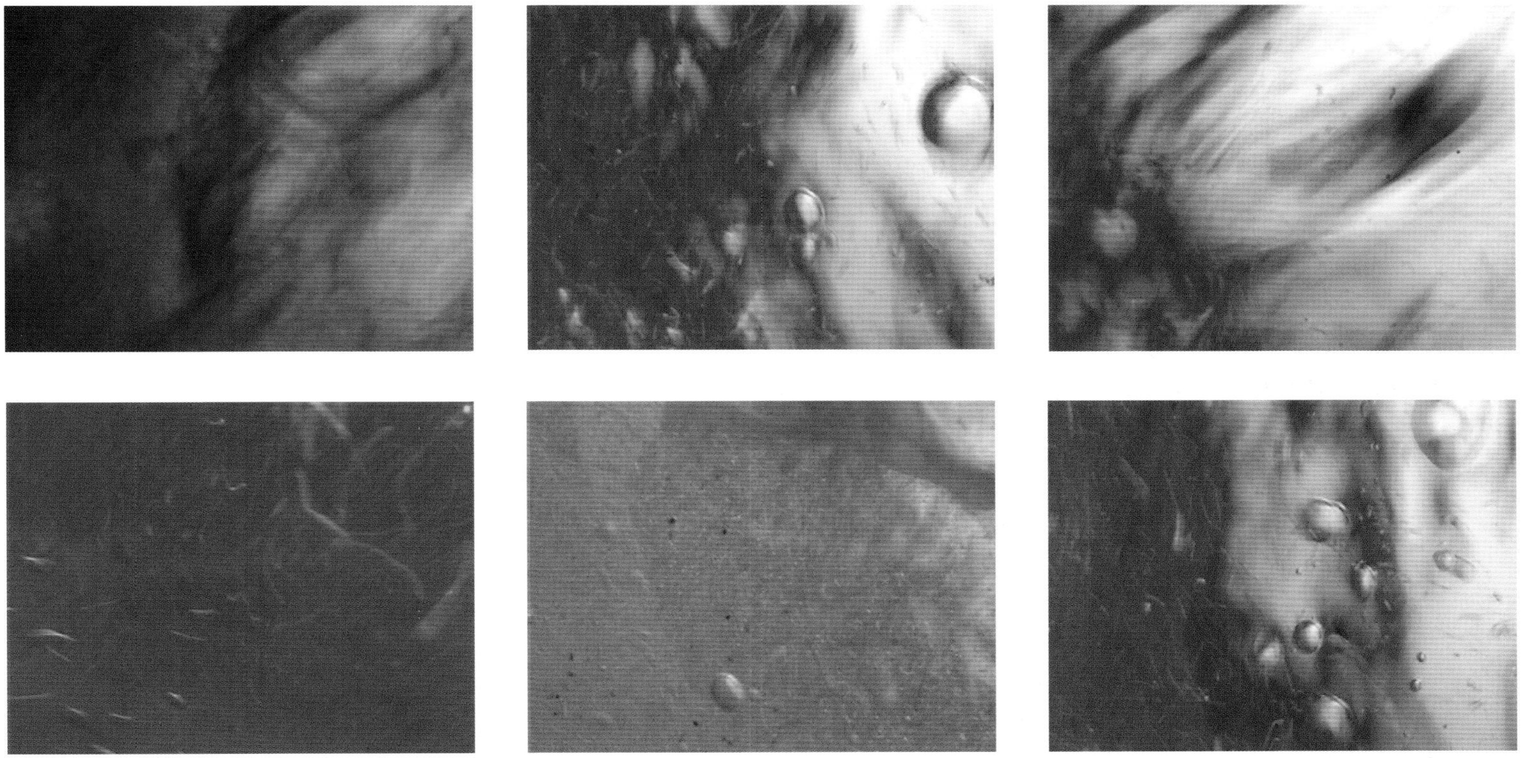

In An Atlantic Wave 2006, Video © the Artist

Jessica Cooper

Jessica Cooper has been eliminating colour in her recent paintings, paring down the representation of objects and vessels to form, tone and line against a shallow recessive space. Brought up in Trevowan near Morvah and now living in Pendeen, her works seem to contain within them all the spare, wind-blasted and gloriously weather-worn aspects of those ancient landscapes, down to the simplest of forms. Using a line that remains structural within the work is important to Cooper, but in some instances her line seems to have a narrative, a palimpsest of something else within it.

That they do not appear to be paintings about the Cornish landscape but rather more an idea of still life is both surprising and mysterious. Such a perceptual shift between landscape as still life and still life as landscape recollects Ben Nicholson's table-top canvases of the 1950s made in Porthmeor Studios. Cooper has always remained interested in achieving both balance and space in her paintings. She is used to layering imagery into her work and then reducing back by using monochromatic black or white and a painting made in this manner may have up to twenty layers applied.

Cooper has a strong, sometimes almost sculptural, sense of design reminiscent particularly of William Scott with whom she shares an affinity for line and categorisation, a graphic feeling for rightness of placement on the canvas surface.

Selected Biography

1967
Born Bristol

1985–6
Foundation Course Diploma,
Falmouth School of Art, Cornwall

1986–9
BA (Hons) Degree Fine Art / Textiles,
Goldsmith's College, London

Selected Solo Exhibitions

2006
Edgarmodern Fine Art, Bath

2004–6
The Stour Gallery, Warwickshire

2003–5
Thompsons Galleries, London
Badcock's Gallery, Cornwall

2001
Newlyn Art Gallery, Newlyn

Selected Group Exhibitions

2006
The Hart Gallery, London
Colour And Chemistry, Sherborne House, Dorset

2005–6
RWA Open Painting Exhibition, Royal West of England Academy, Bristol

2004–6
Martin Tinney Gallery, Cardiff

Awards

2005
Open Painting Exhibition, RWA,
Highly Commended Award
University of the West of England, Drawing Quarters Award

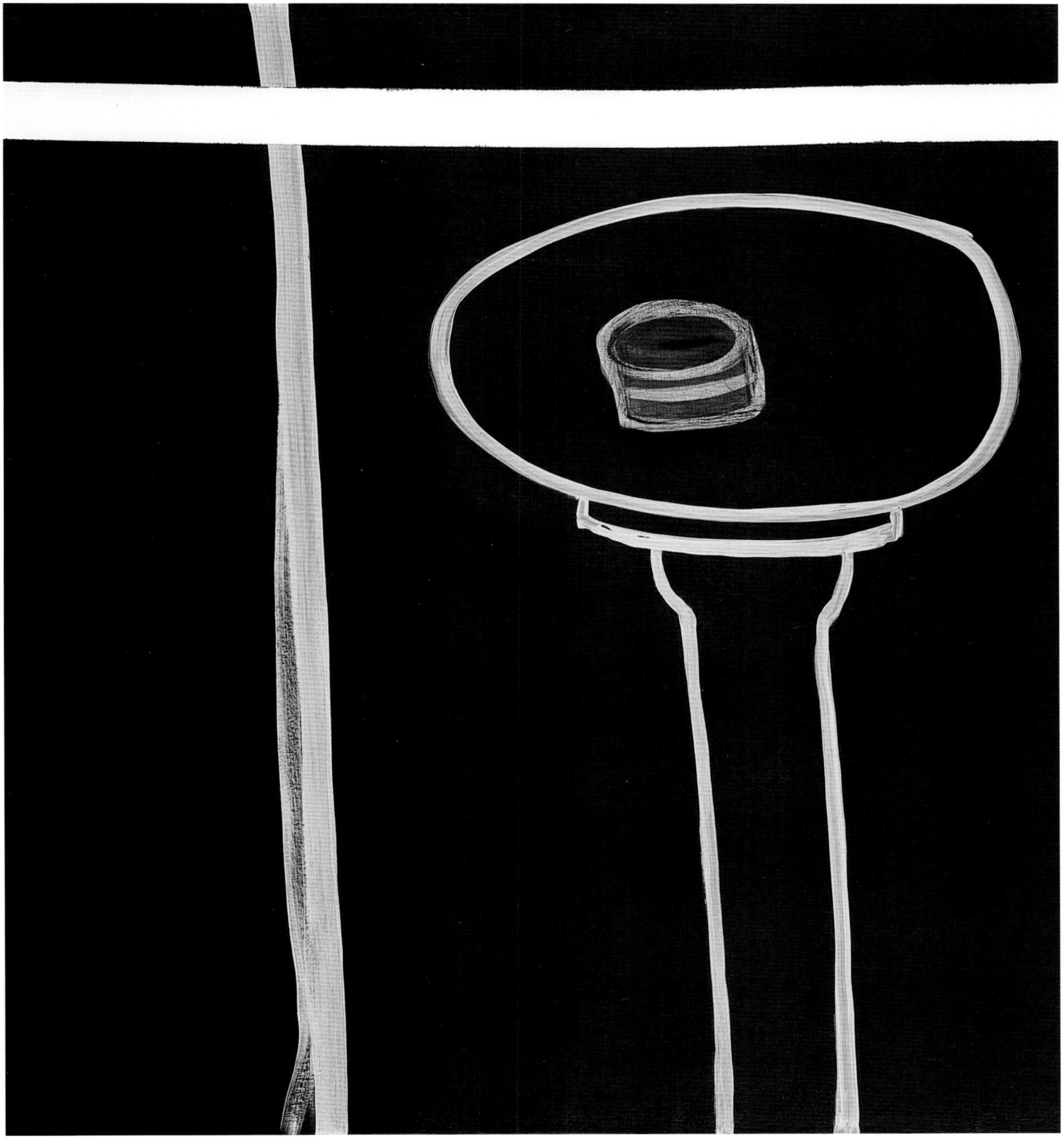

All the things I should have said but didn't 2006, Acrylic and pencil on canvas, 97 x 92 cm © the Artist

Iain Robertson

Iain Robertson has been living and working in Cornwall since 1999, having spent the greater part of his life in Edinburgh. Over the past thirteen years, Robertson has been evolving his vocabulary or sign language of abstract symbols and in early 2006 made a pivotal multiple painting which set out to show something of his lexicon of individual forms. *Mega-Jazzy* 2006, consists of fifty paintings which are one foot square. Unlike his individual paintings which owe a debt to chance and coincidence, where the paint (and motifs) collide and overlap on a rich and heavily worked surface, these small, individual works have a distinctive and jewel-like quality. Within each painting the symbols are rendered simply and directly. They can be examined by the artist within their own space and without the extensive layering of paint and colour of the textured surface seen in previous works.

What is interesting about this revolutionary exercise is that the artist has had an opportunity to scrutinise individual forms – in different positions – and learn more about his intuitive processes. That the individual paintings may be placed in any configuration, results in a huge number of rich juxtapositions within the final painting. This creates the possibility of seeing anew the vocabulary that Robertson has been working with for a number of decades.

Mega-Jazzy has created something of a watershed in Robertson's practice and the painting *Poet's Love, Series II, No I* 2006, is one of a new series of works to emerge after its construction. Allowing the simple fluidity of paint to drip and splatter in a joyous evocation of the action, two triangulated forms balance harmoniously in a shallow pictorial space. Complementary colours heighten each other signalling a new and brave departure.

Selected Biography

1955
Born Cyprus

1978–9
Cumbria College of Art and Design

1979–82
Exeter College of Art and Design

Selected Solo Exhibitions

2006
Fifty at Fifty, Lemon Street Gallery, Truro

2001
New Paintings, Art First, London

Selected Group Exhibitions

2007
Behind Appearances, Scottish Painting and the Modern Movement, City Arts Centre, Edinburgh

2006
London Contemporary Art Fair
Lemon Street Gallery, Truro

2005
Paske, Galerie Moderne, Silkeborg, Denmark
Lemon Street Gallery, Truro

2004
Print Open, Royal West of England Academy, Bristol
Paske, Galerie Moderne Silkeborg Denmark
Lemon Street Gallery, Truro
St Ives *Next Wave* The Hutson Gallery, London

2003
Art First in Print, Art First, London
Paske, Galerie Moderne, Silkeborg Denmark
Lemon Street Gallery, Truro

Collections

Standard Life; University of Minnesota; Grizedale Society Cumbria; Paintings in Hospitals (Scotland); Cornwall County Council Schools Art Collection

Selected Awards

2005
Arts Council of England

1988
Pollock Krasner Foundation New York

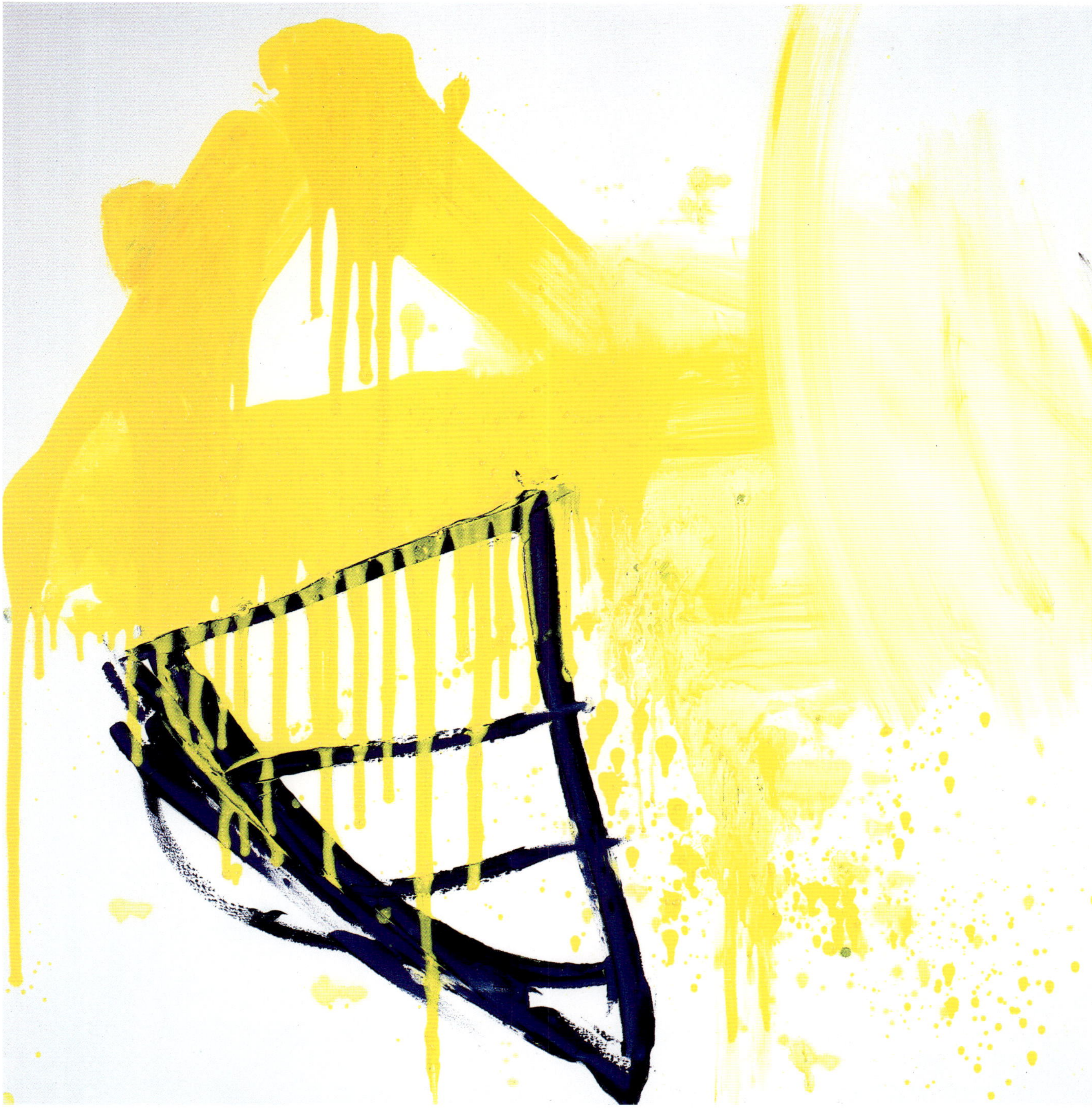

Poet's Love Series II No I 2006, Oil on canvas 90 x 90 cm © the Artist

Clare Wardman

Inspired by the quality of light in St Ives where she has had a studio since 1999, Clare Wardman's new work comes from a series of drawings begun in 2003. *Prima Vista* 25 August 2005, has evolved from *Light Drawings* 2003, a series of works on paper, which tracked the movement of daylight in her studio. Her question for the work was to discover how the physical movement of sunlight and the transformation of the surface it came into contact with, could be expressed in the medium of drawing and painting. She is fascinated by the 100 minutes of external sunlight which passes through the skylight of her studio and in observing and recording the subtle or dramatic changes (always variable due to the weather systems which affect it).

Wardman is interested in the idea that the studio environment itself can create a climate for the artist's cognitive processes and intuitive actions. In working with the restrictions set for her by the aperture of the window above and the position of the studio in relation to the sun, she found herself responding repeatedly, on an emotional and intellectual level, to a diamond form which moved across the surface of the canvas triptych she was painting. This has set up questions in her mind about the secular nature of the subject matter – light and shadow and its symbiotic relationship with religions – light and dark (in terms of a classical allegory).

Like Roger Hilton before her, Wardman is interested in exploring the use of charcoal on bare canvas to investigate its vivacious energy and emotional resonance. And, inspired by the processes of Patrick Heron in his large canvases of the 1970s, she is working with small brush marks to make this new series of paintings. Working in this way the artist is noting how her paintings evolve in order to understand her own visual vocabulary of marks, strokes and gestures.

The *Light Painting* series represents these experiments with plastic surfaces and illuminated pictorial spaces, where a balance and tension of line with painterly marks is achieved. Her aim is to arrive close to an image which alludes to time without being set in time.

Selected Biography

1960
Born Yorkshire

1982
BA (Hons) Fine Art Painting,
Exeter College of Art and Design

Group Exhibitions

2007
Behind Appearances Scottish Painting And The Modern Movement, City Arts Centre, Edinburgh, Scotland

2006
100 Years of Penwith Art Porthminster Gallery, St Ives

2002–6
Open studios, St Ives September Festival, Sail Loft Studios, St Ives

2005
Rwa Open Painting Exhibition, Highly Commended, Royal West of England, Academy Bristol

2004
150th Celebration of Excellence in Art and Design at Exeter College of Art and Design
Porthmeor Belgrave Gallery, St Ives
St Ives Next Wave Hutson Gallery, London

2003
Summer Exhibition, Lemon Street Gallery, Truro
Winter Exhibition, Penwith Gallery, St Ives

Collections

University of Minnesota Medical Centre, USA; Scottish Arts Council; Grizedale Society Grizedale Sculpture Park; Bayer Plc Head Office; PIHS Painting In Hospitals, Scotland; Cornwall County Council Schools Art Collection

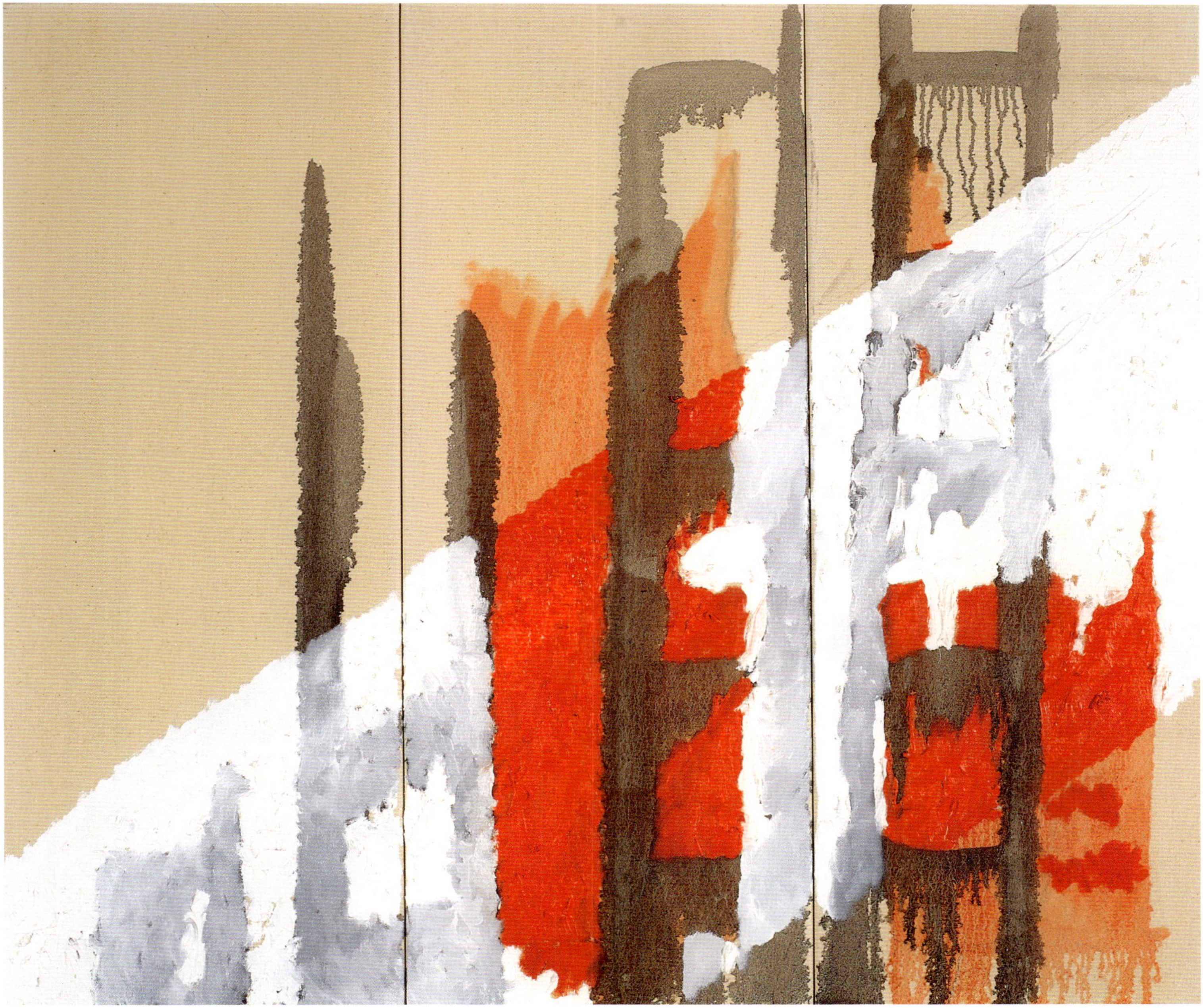

Prima Vista 25 August 2005 (Light Tracking) 2005, Oil on canvas, 76 x 91 cm © the Artist

Richard Nott

Richard Nott has a sculptural preoccupation with the material world but draws his inspiration not – as you might imagine – from nature but from the utilitarian industrial materials that, for many, would constitute a rather dull aesthetic reality, such as building work and house renovation. Sculpture that is made accumulatively from industrial material – although not in an industrial format – does have a utilitarian reality (think of the bricks of Carl Andre for example). There is a real danger of formatting such things as sculpture in this manner because of the relationship between it and the convention of the industrial production systems that are used in a building context. If you plan to use plasterboard for example, the manner in which the material is treated has to be perverted from the normal utilitarian use and this is the route an artist might take towards a sculptural reality and away from an industrialised reality.

But Nott's objective is not to make dumb material express human emotions and thoughts. Rather than projecting his intelligence into using one material as a subterfuge, or to transform it for another purpose, he elects to operate within an alternative convention. This is the convention of the painted object we know as paintings. But this object, *Striation (A)* 2005, which looks like a painting, is in fact a sculpture. Sculptures that are based on repetition and stacking provide an opportunity to experience the very substance of the material (if you can recognise it) in a primary form. Working with objects which have this kind of layering gives us an opportunity to experience a new set of questions as the objects begin to have a special relationship or dialogue – in architectural terms – with the space they occupy. They set up questions of scale, repetition, tempo, surface and geometry, marks and their meaning and, of course, colour.

What is surprising about the *Stratum Series* is just how delicate they seem to be. The process of stacking is an elementary construction principle and therefore these works ought to be close to archetypes of primary structures. But the artist has evoked the mutability of the material to present another metaphoric possibility and provoked our imaginative response to ask what might seem to be an unusual question. What lies beneath?

Selected Biography

1963
Born Cornwall

1983–5
BA Fine Arts,
Lancashire Polytechnic

1987–9
MA Fine Arts,
Reading

Solo Exhibitions

2007
Gallon Viewpoing Gallery, PCAD, Plymouth

2006
Richard Nott at Dean Clough, Halifax

2005
Platform 102 Gallery, Tea Building, London

2003
New Millenium Gallery, St Ives

2001
Transitions Newlyn Art Gallery, Newlyn

Selected Group Exhibitions

2007
The St Ives School 1997–2007 Howard Gardens Gallery, Cardiff

Richard Nott, Sax Impey, Sam Hall, Andy Hughes, Andy Whall, Graham Gaunt

2001
Richard Nott, Sax Impey, Ged Quinn, Fermyn Woods Contemporary Art, Kettering

Awards

1994
South West Arts visual arts award

Residencies

12th International Weeks of Painting, Slovenia – 12 Artists from Europe working in Slovenia, work produced exhibited in Slovenia and Austria

Collections

Slaughter and May, London and Hong Kong; Leleia Foundation, Slovenia; Private collections

Striation (A) 2005, Mixed media on panel, 153 x 153 x 6 cm © the Artist

Luke Frost

The pristine surfaces of these architectonic paintings bear the hallmarks of American post-Abstraction and conceptual practice as they nod in the direction of Barnett Newman and the Minimalist sculptor Dan Flavin; but there the affinity with both artists ends. Up to ten layers of paint – dependent upon Luke Frost's selection of colour or tone – results in a surface that recedes into sometimes deep, sometimes shallow, recessive space. Held in place by one, sometimes two electric 'zips' or 'volts' of contrasting colours that are painted illusionistically, these ostensibly flat areas of painted surface essentially deceive the eye and mind to expand into space which surrounds the canvas.

In terms of scale, the paintings in the *Volt Series* do not envelope the viewer with colour or texture or tone. Instead, they operate a 'push-pull' as they sit within architectural contexts creating a window of opportunity for the eye. They also have a sculptural relationship with the body in terms of the extent of the gaze at relatively close quarters. Frost has in the past experimented with installations using fluorescent tubes and is clearly exploring how the human eye registers or is affected by colour in association with colour and how an image may be retained by the retina on looking away from the painting.

These abstract paintings imply space rather than define it through their mass and surface, and the juxtaposition of contrasting colour hints at a relationship with nature. Working within the legacy of the St Ives School of Modernists, Frost is attempting to relate colour and form to create a space sensation that has, at its heart, a representational experience that is devoid of gesture and authorship.

Selected Biography

1976
Born Penzance, Cornwall

1994–5
Foundation In Art and Design,
Falmouth College of Arts

1995–8
BA (Hons) Fine Art,
Bath

Solo Exhibitions

2006
The Somerville Gallery, Plymouth

2003
The Somerville Gallery, Plymouth
Badcocks Gallery, Newlyn

Selected Group Exhibitions

2005
The Strand Gallery, Aldeburgh
The Somerville Gallery, Plymouth

2004
The City Gallery, London
Spectrum Gallery, London (2 person)
The Affordable Art Fair with Badcocks Gallery,
New York

2003
Xposure Artist Led Group Show, Gallery
Space, Penzance

Collections

The Bank of America

Artist in Residence

2007–8
Tate St Ives

Volts No 7 2006, Acrylic on canvas, 152.5 x 152.5 cm, On loan Somerville Gallery, Plymouth © the Artist

Anthony Frost

The collage paintings of Anthony Frost have compositional tension in that texture, form and colour are held in a balanced relationship of abstract shapes. Frost speaks of the need to be in a state of mind where opportunities offered by chance, coincidence and intuition can be taken advantage of, where a sense of 'rightness' may be achieved. What he is speaking of is a sense of 'flow' a mood induced by deep internal concentration – often aided by listening to music – whereby the intuitive processes of the brain become dominant over the rational and predictive. Where the desire to plan or order the structure of the painting is held in check by instinct and imagination.

Frost often works with the contradictory energies of 'push' and 'pull' created by the painting's structure where flat shapes of colour are held in planar space. Whilst we may read these shapes as flat space, openings or emerging forms in the painting's surface, we also see colour as a point of vibrant tension where the architectural weight or placement of pure colour seems to be for the eye only.

Frost's paintings however, are not random acts, accidents of nature or slips made between brush and hand. There are repeated structural forms in the paintings of the past five years. A regular occurrence is that of a narrow truncated triangle – almost like a sail form – that appears to be placed on its side. This dramatic shape holds colour poised within and outside of it, in a rhythm which mimics the absolute in geometry's dynamic. In the new painting in this exhibition *Surface Noise* 2006, there is an evolution in Frost's vocabulary of forms. Geometry is modified and fractured, the edges are softer and colour has been selectively reduced from its earlier complexity. This painting is heavily collaged with thick canvas and cord but the vivacious treatment of paint is a joyous response to the breaking geometry of the form and highlights the asymmetric and irregular components within its structure.

Selected Biography

1951
Born St Ives, Cornwall

1970–3
BA (Hons) Fine Art,
Cardiff College of Art

Selected Solo Exhibitions

2007
Surface Noise, Beaux Arts, London
Surface Noise – The Prints, Royal Albert Memorial Museum, Exeter

2005
The Otter Gallery, Chichester University
Lunar Notes – Neon Dreams, Advanced Graphics, London

2004
Zig Zag Wanderer, The Somerville Gallery, Plymouth

2003
Big colour in Space, Space, Penzance

Collections

Nuffield Trust; John Moores; Contemporary Art Society; Cornwall County Council; Royal Cornwall Museum and Art Gallery, Truro; The Kasser Foundation, New York; Devon County Council; The Contemporary Irish Art Society; Limmerick Art Gallery and Museum, Ireland; Whitworth Gallery, Manchester; Lloyds TSB, London; Kings College, Cambridge; Addenbrooks Hospital, Cambridge; St Georges Hospital, London; The Bank of America, London

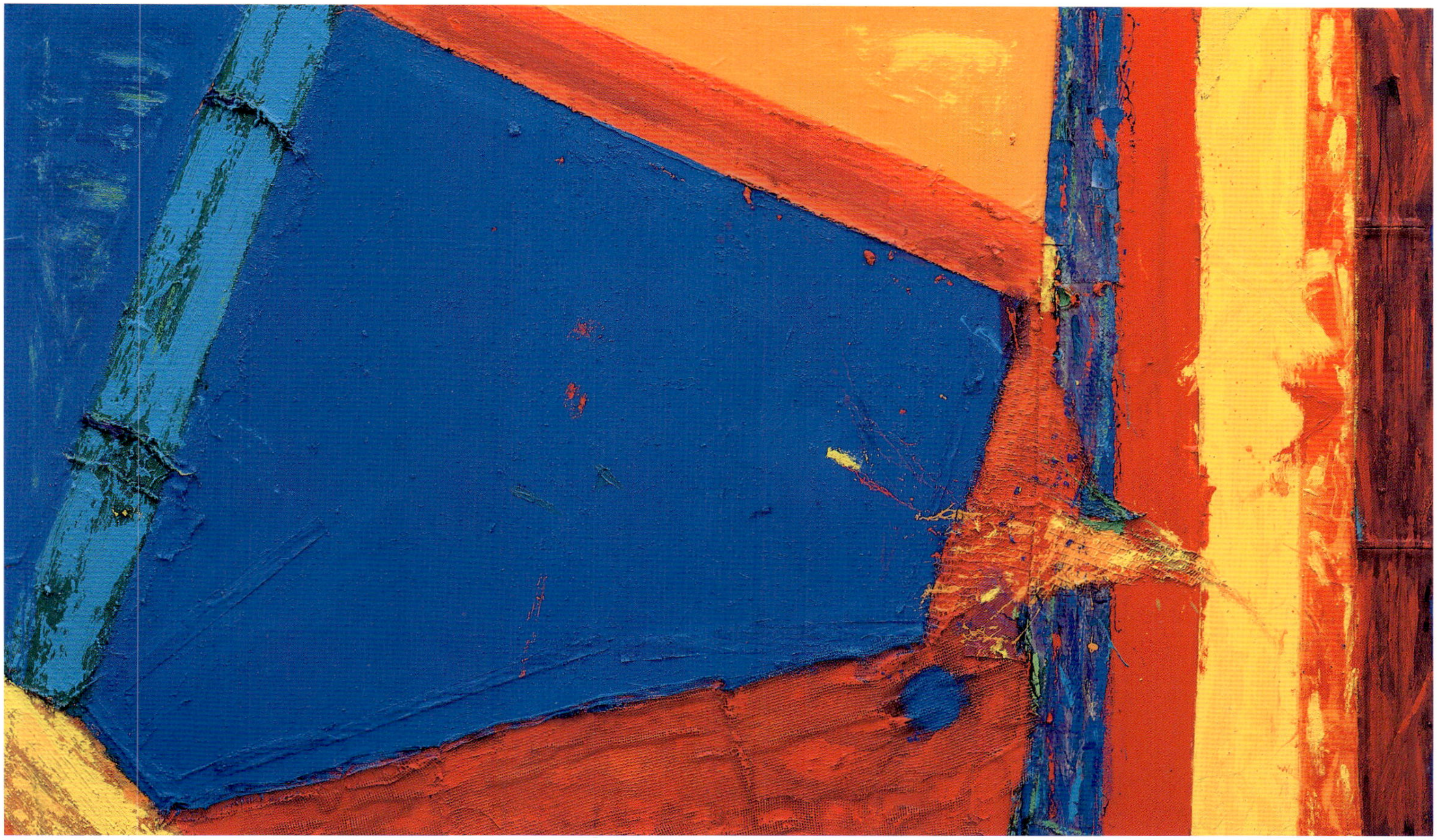

Surface Noise (when it blows it stacks) 2006, Acrylic and collage on canvas, 121.9 x 210.8 cm © the Artist

Hadrian Pigott

The video *Rifiuti* 2005, is a mesmeric kaleidoscope, hypnotic and relaxing. We can enjoy the constant dance of these objects as if they had a life and intent of their own. The images of the bottles and footballs are vibrant and positive, but nagging questions occur too. The video describes a modern phenomena of plastic detritus cast adrift by the inhabitants of Rome into a weir with a strong backwash that traps all the objects. This phenomena was observed on the River Tiber's journey through the city. Jars, bottles, blocks of polystyrene, footballs and bottle tops dance and jostle in a ceaseless self-cleansing turmoil, a turbulent but rich tide of colour and form. Interestingly, the materials and forms appear to self-categorise as they become entrapped in the whirling eddies of water. As if to miraculously escape the inevitable downward suction of a whirlpool, now and then, a number of bottle tops and jars (often the lightest in weight), will become detached from the main crowd of objects and sail out jauntily only to be drawn back to the original group and tumbled back into position with the rest of the material – the plastic refuse of contemporary life.

What are we to make of this film with its casual appearance but aesthetic solidarity of plastic forms arranging themselves in entertaining loops and arabesques? There are many ways to think about this work. Is this perhaps a romanticised take on consumption taken to excess? (Rome in July is obviously a thirsty place). Is it a comment on the hidden systems of food production and distribution? Or could it be that *Rifiuti* is a simple celebration of a moment of beauty glimpsed in between the grandeur and history that permeates the city? Think of the plastic bag floating on eddies above the suburban road at the beginning of the Alan Ball/Sam Mendes film *American Beauty* and the ominous artificiality that it portends in light of the storm to come. Recollect Tony Cragg's wall sculpture entitled *Britain seen from the North* 1981, which depicts a life-sized figure observing a large scheme of Britain on its side, comprising multi-coloured plastic detritus from the River Thames.

Since the early 1990s, Pigott's sculptures have been concerned with the excesses and ills of consumer society, such as *Dysfunction* and *Submersives*, (I & II), a series of body-sized amorphous soap sculptures which simultaeneously attract and repel. More recently, he made a work called *TAT Modern Britain* in which attractive industrial foam pebbles from the wreck of the RMS Mulhiem at Lands End were sample-bagged and exhibited and sold to raise funds for Surfers Against Sewage. In the sparkling Atlantic Ocean outside Tate St Ives is possibly where the beautiful rubbish from the Tiber will end up as microscopic fragments too tiny to see and which will be absorbed by all creatures who inhabit the ocean or live by its means.

Selected Biography

1961
Born Aldershot, Hampshire

1980–3
BSc Geology,
Exeter University

1990–3
MA Sculpture,
Royal College of Art

1992
Eduardo Paolozzi Travel Scholarship

2004–5
Project Artist on *Elements of Drawing*,
Ashmolean Museum

Selected Solo Exhibitions

2005
RIFIUTI Wordsworth Trust, Cumbria

2000
Galeria Marabini, Bologna

1998
Hypergienics Victoria Miro Gallery, London
Another Place James van Damme Gallery, Brussels

Selected Group Exhibitions

2006
Modern Art @ Potteries Museum, Arts Council collection, Stoke-on-Trent

2005
Darkening Folds – Dazzling Strangeness
Ashmolean Museum

1997
Clean & Sane Maria Lind, edsvik, Sweden
Sensation Young British Artists from the Saatchi Collection, Royal Academy London
A Changed World British Council, touring Pakistan, South Africa, Cyprus

1996
Reternity National Museum of Sweden, Stockholm

1995
Fetishism: Visualising Power and Desire touring exhibition, South Bank Centre
Young British Artists V Saatchi Gallery, London

1994
BT New Contemporaries touring UK exhibition
Art Unlimited: Multiples of the '60s and '90s
Arts Council touring exhibition

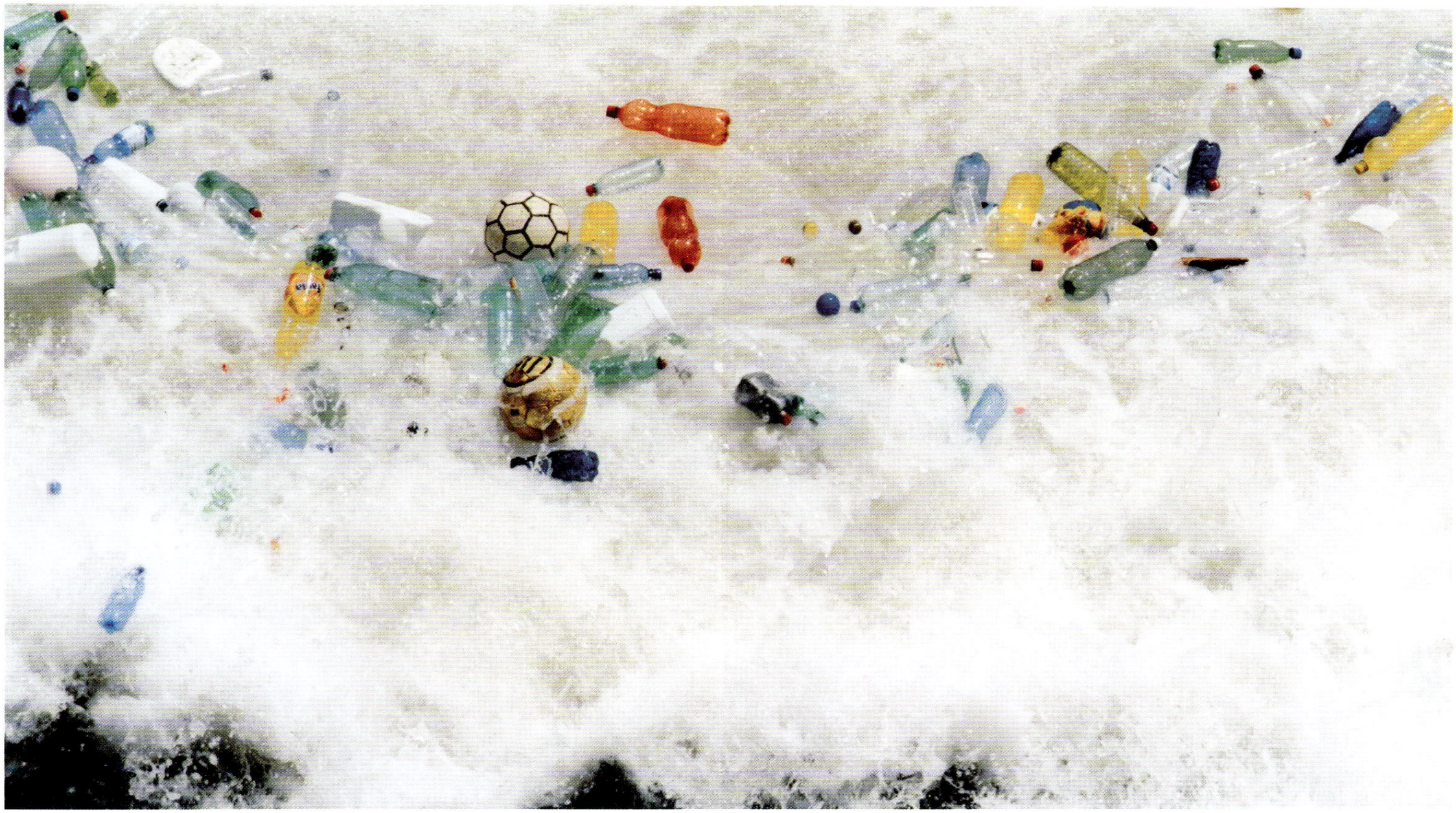

Rifiuti 2005, Video, © the Artist

Neil Canning

The paintings of Neil Canning seem to be evolving somewhere in that area of tension between figurative and abstract art. Gestural abstraction in the sweeps and swathes of thick, smudged and glazed patches of colour often have an urgent, expressive quality. These strokes of colour are not only evidence of the action of the material on the canvas, but the paint appears to evoke the pictorial techniques used by artists to describe the powerful aspects of the natural world and its weather systems which we can find in the epic narrative paintings of the late nineteenth century. In a relatively small painting such as *Shine* 2006 there seems to be a response to the scale, dynamics and textures of the elements encompassed in what is, ostensibly, an image brought into being through intuitive abstraction.

As Canning continues to evolve his language of forms, he identifies an affinity with a number of modernist artists who were working in St Ives, particularly Peter Lanyon, Patrick Heron and Barbara Hepworth and, like many artists before him, works through formal relationships inspired by key works of those artists. He draws inspiration from the air and sea, creating an idea of beauty through an emotional engagement in the classic tradition that any relationship between artist and viewer would entail. In many of his recent paintings, seen in his studio in St Ives, Canning has constructed a formal, visual abstract language using amorphous forms such as roughly drawn circles and spots, explosions of colour and intersecting lines to suggest landscape structures affected by great winds and atmospheres.

It is a world in constant flux – a moving world – in a ceaseless state of gleam and glow, air and transparency. In the combination of shape, line, colour and gesture, Canning, like his illustrious predecessors in the St Ives School, considers the nature of space, manipulating the reading of colour and line as form in relation to it and the transient realm of the natural world.

Selected Biography

1960
Born Oxfordshire

Solo Exhibitions

2006
Portland Gallery, London

2000–6
New Millennium Gallery, St Ives

2005
Martin Tinney Gallery, Cardiff

2004
Advanced Graphics, London

2003
Lowry Hotel, Manchester
Lynne Strover Gallery, Cambridge

Selected Group Exhibitions

2006
Royal Academy Summer Exhibition (regular exhibitor since 1981)
Original Print Gallery, Dublin
ISPDA Print Fair, New York
Castlegate House Gallery, Cockermouth, Cumbria

2003
West Cork Arts Centre, Skibbereen, Ireland

Selected Collections

Ashmolean Museum; Bank of England; Credit Suisse; ICI; British Embassy, Venezuela; H.M. Customs and Excise; London Hospitals Trust; National Westminster Bank; Rolls Royce; University of Exeter; United Nations, New York

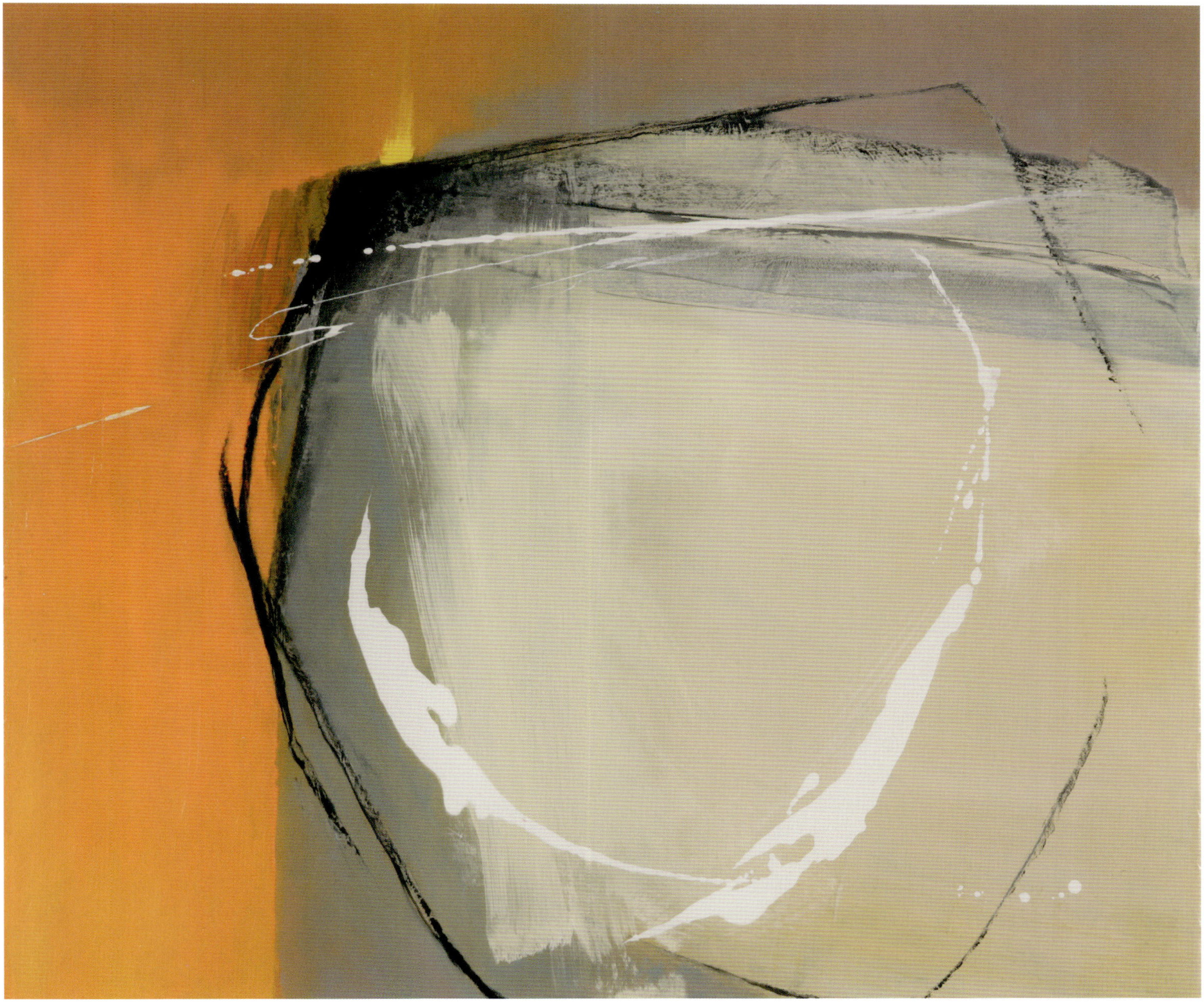

Shine 2006, Oil on canvas, 76 x 91 cm, Collection Mr and Mrs A W Wright © the Artist

Sax Impey

Sax Impey has described the process of making his paintings as a synthesis of mapping or charting the territory of his thoughts, never knowing exactly where he will end up in a painting. In the past six years he has been interested in collecting lottery data, sub-nuclear physics and the decay of sub-atomic particles, aerial reconnaissance charts, medieval maps, mathematics, and interpretative strategies. The paintings he has made have often presented an image concealed within an image, as if he preferred not to embrace an austere interpretation of mathematical data and instead, chose to frame it within an imaginative and mysterious non-place.

It is true that a carefully calibrated grid based on mathematical data might serve as a reference point to be subverted in this way. However, to speak of references is to impose logic upon Impey's imagery that does not sit well with the cognitive wanderings during which these paintings are made. In *Event 9* 2005, Impey has used spirals and lines which strike upwards and across the canvas – elements that call associations in our mind of ancient maritime charts and weather systems, or even recall the layered paintings of Wilhelmina Barns-Graham of fractured ice such as *Variations on a Theme (Splintered Ice No 2)* 1987. In Impey's painting lines hover in a deep recessive space where the light appears to fall evenly, fostering the illusion of an aerial space in the centre of the painting, where the eye is pulled into a distance beyond the surface.

However, flatness is emphasised too in the structuring of the work; painting, reducing back by sanding the painting's surface and repainting the image. This layering seems to induce a sense of the temporal as much as it does the spatial, reminding us of Naum Gabo's exquisite ability to capture the indwelling forces of natural matter.

Selected Biography

1969
Born Penzance, Cornwall

1988–91
BA (Hons) Fine Art, Newport

Solo Exhibitions

2005
Catena OneOTwo Gallery, London

2004
Events New Millennium Gallery, St Ives

2002
Labyrinths New Millennium Gallery, St Ives

2000
Transition Newlyn Art Gallery, Newlyn

Selected Group Exhibitions

2006
Fragments Cafe Gallery Projects, London and Tom Thompson Gallery, Owen Sound, Canada

2003
Starting a Collection Art First Contemporary Art, London

2002
Constructed Newlyn Art Gallery, Newlyn

2001
Sax Impey, Richard Nott, Ged Quinn Fermyn Woods Contemporary Art, Kettering

2000
Ark 2000 Dilston Grove Church, London

1997
Kunstbrucke Dock 11, Berlin
Landmarks Cafe Gallery Projects, London

Residencies

1997
Kunstbrucke Berlin

Collections

Arts Council Collection; Warwick University; Private collections

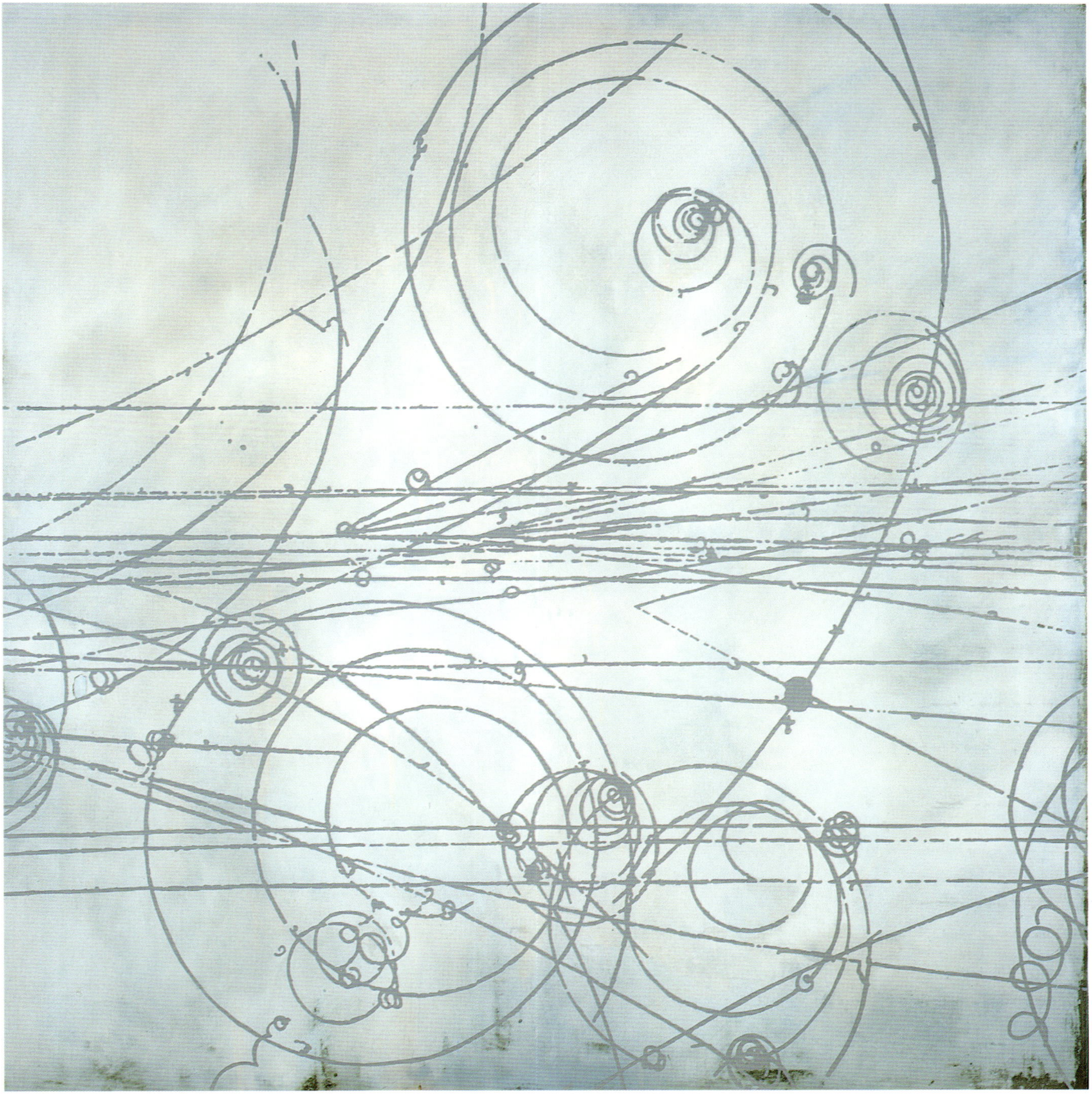

Event 9 2005, Mixed media on wood, 204 x 204 cm © the Artist

Jesse Leroy Smith

The paintings of Jesse Leroy Smith explore the subtlety of colour and touch in the way that the oil paint is applied in thin washes to the canvas surface giving the fluid spontaneity of watercolour paint. Smith trained at the Royal Academy Schools, London and since moving to Cornwall has been exploring different forms of mark making such as pouring, burning, sanding, carving and staining. Having decided to make oil paintings with a similar economy and urgency to watercolour paint, he has been using his family – particularly his six year old son – as subject matter. Smith is looking for a subtle humour alongside a religious devotion to the figure or portrait. His paintings develop through a process of building up and stripping down the relationship between image and surface, resulting in an enigmatic trace that has something of an historic atmosphere.

Smith has travelled extensively, drawing from works of antiquity in a variety of contexts, including the Giotto Chapel in Padua and the Academia Collection, Venice as a means of engaging with the full potential of the human image. He has an affinity with the works of Giotto, Leon Golub and William Kentridge amongst other artists. Smith will also use video stills and photography to source images, from which he will make a series of drawings to take them to another level of expression. He also makes many drawings from life in a rapid and economical manner to capture transitory moments as essential methods to discover images, rather than contriving them.

The painting in this exhibition *Leopard* 2006, has something of the atmosphere of Renaissance portraiture circa 1400. At this moment in art history, a landscape is portrayed through a window behind the figure and the subject of the portrait looks directly at the viewer, whilst resting a hand against a surface placed up to the picture plane of the canvas. Clad in a leopard skin, the figure appears self-possessed, knowing, all powerful and iconic, a heroic image of innocence. In his work Smith appears to be repeatedly assessing the discrepancy between uniformity and individual identity, and instead is creating an image of myth and power.

Selected Biography

1966
Born London

1989–92
MA in Painting,
Royal Academy Schools, London
BA (Hons) in Fine Art,
Norwich School of Art, Norfolk
Foundation Course,
East Ham, London

Selected Solo Exhibitions

2007
Royal Academy of Arts, Café Gallery, London
Goldfish Contemporary Fine Art, Penzance

2005
Transition, Newlyn Art Gallery, Newlyn

2001
Reign One Gallery, London

Selected Group Exhibitions

2006
Cross Gallery, Dublin
Goldfish Contemporary Fine Art, Penzance
McHardy Coombes, Tower Bridge, London

2004–6
Lemon Street Gallery, Truro

1996–2006
Royal Academy Summer Exhibition, London

1998–2005
Roman Black Gallery, London
BowWow, London

2005
Belgrave Gallery, St Ives
Royal West of England, Bristol, Open Painting Exhibition

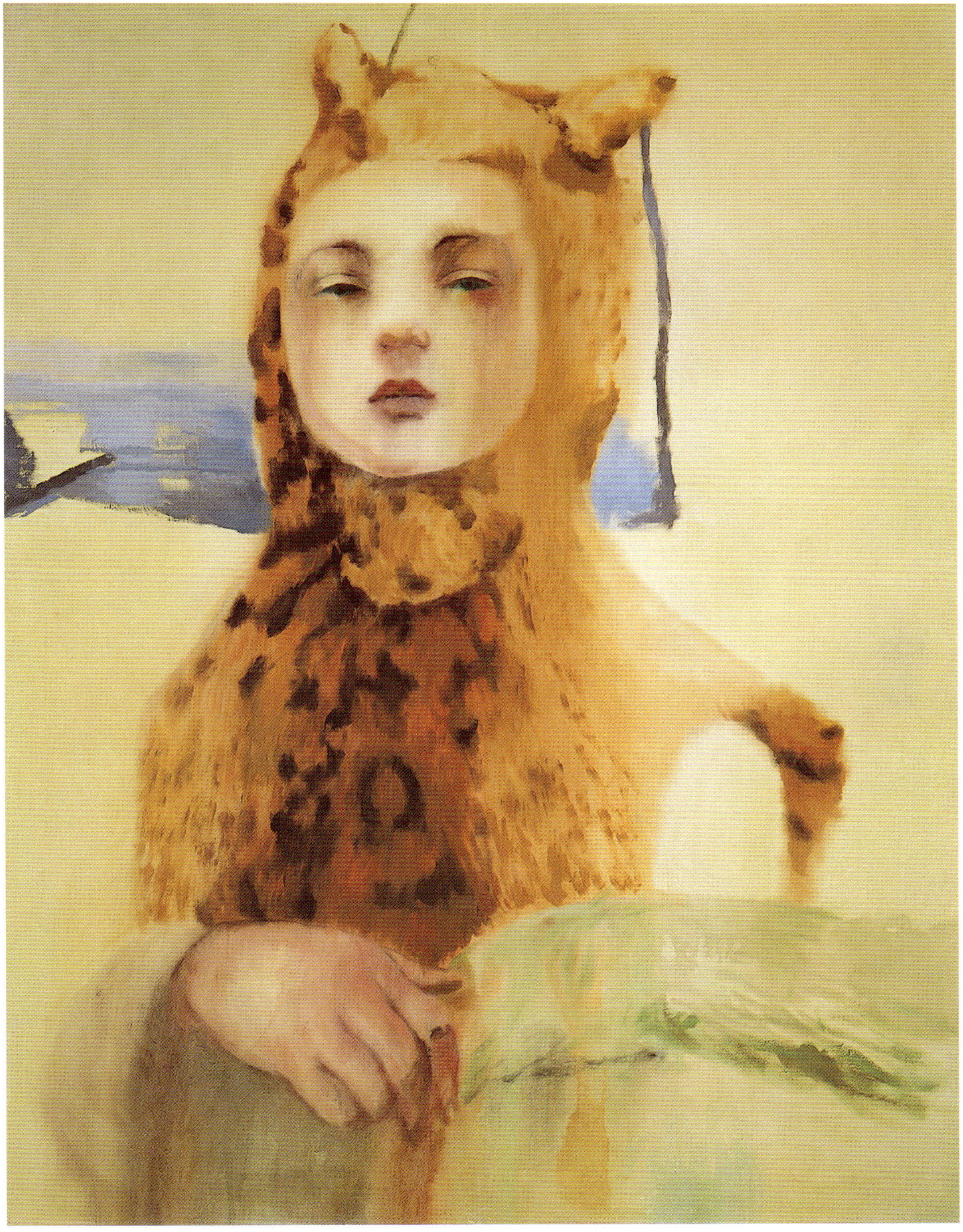

Leopard 2006, Oil on canvas, 178 x 140 cm © the Artist

Ged Quinn

In *Asleep by the Light of Glow-worms* 2005, Quinn samples a work by the German artist Caspar David Friedrich titled *Sea of Ice* 1823–5. The image, an imagined real event, sees the 'wreck' as a Romantic symbol, but a secondary symbol. This is incidental to the over-wrought and fractured landscape into which Quinn places the cinematic version of HG Wells' novel *The Time Machine*. The story finds the protagonist, taken by love, travelling through time to rescue a future race of humans, apparently living in a utopian existence, but in reality being nothing more than farm animals harvested regularly by an underground race of Morlocks.

This time machine is occupied by the German artist Joseph Beuys (1921–86). Beuys was most famous for his public performances and championing a universal sense of human creativity. Quinn shows him in the midst of *How to explain pictures to a dead hare* 1965. His face is covered in honey and gold leaf, an iron slab attached to his boot. In his arms he cradles a dead hare into the ear of which he mumbles/whispers explanations of the pictures that (in the performance) lined the walls.

Quinn, in his inimitable fashion plays with the codified meanings of everyday objects 'made strange' and the symbols of both a Romantic and post-modern European culture to bathetic effect; honey and gold – utopian society and alchemy, the Romantic idea of the sublime juxtaposed with twentieth century cinematic cliché. Beuys is central, but sidelined in scale.

Beuysian imagery gently permeates the grandiose (un)natural backdrop. The markings of Beuys' plane (JU87) in which he famously crashed in the Crimea in 1943 are shown on the wreck intimating the talk which Beuys gave in 1979 of his recollected rescue by Tartars. With all of its echoes of a romantic idea or near death experience and rescue, resulting in mythical and shamanistic powers, it seems like a man waking from an opium dream or viewing the 1970s TV show 'The Champions'. As love took the protagonist of the time machine to the (dys)topian existence of future humanity, so Quinn casts Beuys as a mythical figure travelling through time to right the ills of our lived experience.

Selected Biography

1963
Born Liverpool

1981–4
Ruskin School of Drawing, Oxford

1985–7
Slade School of Fine Art

1988–90
Kunstakademie Dusseldorf

1993–4
Rijksakademie Amsterdam

Selected Solo Exhibitions

2005
Wilkinson Gallery, London
The Heavenly Machine Spike Island, Bristol

2004
Utopia Dystopia Tate St Ives

Selected Group Exhibitions

2007
Salon Nouveau Engholm Engelhorn, Vienna

2005–6
big, small, white works from the Cartin Collection, Hartford, Connecticut. Walton Ford, Glen Ligon, Ged Quinn, Christopher Orr, Wolfgang Laib, Sol Lewitt.

2005
Wonderings… Waugh and Thistleton. Sean Dower, Judith Goddard, Peter Macdonald, Ged Quinn
showCASe City Art Centre, Talbot Rice Gallery Edinburgh
The Real Ideal Millennium Galleries, Sheffield. Gregory Crewdson, Pipilotti Rist, Paul Noble, Cornelia Parker, Ged Quinn, Diana Thater, Mr and Mrs Ivan Morison.

Collections

Tate, London; Victoria and Albert Museum, London; Saatchi Collection, London; Olbricht Collection, Essen Germany; Cartin Collection, USA; Honart Museum, Tehran; Sunderland Museum, UK; Esmee Fairbairn Foundation, London; Private collections

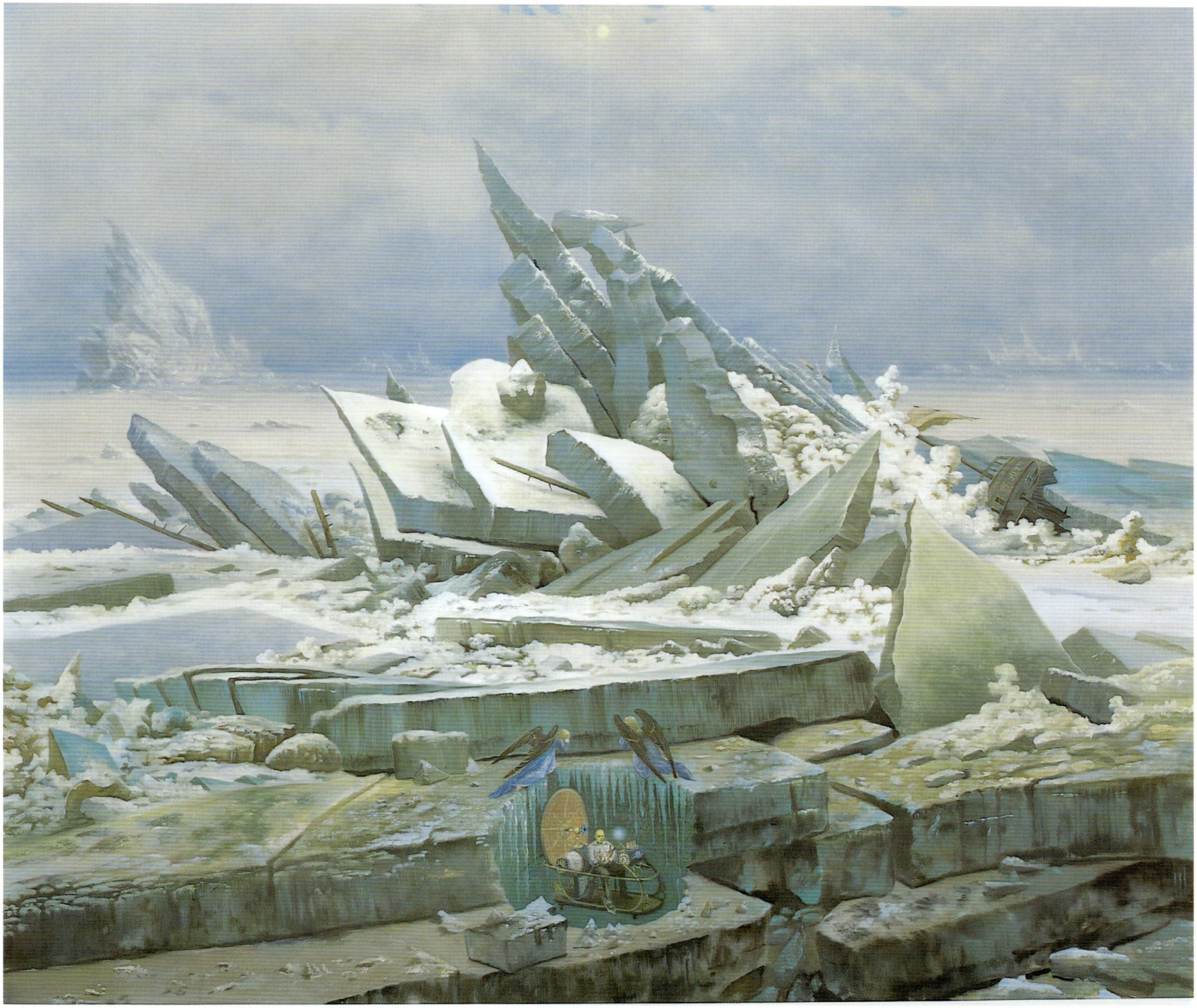

Asleep by the Light of Glow-worms 2005, Oil on linen, 183 x 220 cm, Private collection © the Artist Courtesy Wilkinson Gallery, London

Richard Cook

In his recent paintings Richard Cook evokes a drama of epic proportions to create a memory of nature in a chaotic and untamed state. Walking and drawing on a daily basis are central and the lifeblood of his practice; many sketchbooks and drawings are placed around his studio as he takes information not just from one individual study but several are often pressed into use for the same painting. Cook highlights a number of influences but this new series draws inspiration from Turner and Gainsborough; the vivacious manner in which the paint is applied with texture and fluidity suggests that light permeates both the interior and the surface of the canvas.

Since he began living in Cornwall in 1985, Cook has repeatedly visited the maritime landscapes of Newlyn, Penzance and Lelant and the wild heathlands of Dartmoor. His walks are, more often than not, solitary excursions as he tunes into the isolation of the moment, away from the otherwise dominant pace of daily existence. His paintings describe an illusory passage between the memory of the subject and the moment in time when he – inspired by his response to its beauty and his desire to recreate it – began to draw a version of that experience. The poetry in Cook's work reveals his passion for nature in its most dangerous state – wild, mystical and filled with impending tragedy.

When engaging with his subject he will study the rapid changes of natural light at the ocean's edge. He mentally sketches the writhing surface of the sea and rocks whose surfaces have been shaped and excoriated by the elements. He draws with a vocabulary of forms and lines that have been reduced by continued practice over many years. He does not choose to represent the reality he sees. He observes the inevitable movement of water and drama of clouds suspended in the constantly moving atmospheres. He listens to and surrounds himself with the magnetic powers of earth and sea and creates the object that is the painting.

Selected Biography

1947
Born Cheltenham

1966–70
St Martin's School of Art, London

1970–3
Royal College of Art, London

1985
Moved to Cornwall; living and working in Newlyn

Selected Solo Exhibitions

2006
Art First, London
Lemon Street Gallery, Truro

2001
Tate St Ives

2003, 2000, 1997,1995
Austin/Desmond Fine Art, London

1993
Galerie am Savignyplatz, Berlin

1992
Newlyn Art Gallery, Newlyn

1989
Odette Gilbert Gallery, London

Selected Group Exhibitions

2006
Drawing Inspiration: Contemporary British Drawing Abbot Hall, Kendal

1992
Painting in Cornwall Royal West of England Academy, Bristol

1980
British Art 1940–1980 The Arts Council Collection, Hayward Gallery

1976
The Human Clay Hayward Gallery, London

Selected Awards

2003
Artist's Award, Arts Council, England

2001
Commissions Award, Arts Council, England
Elephant Trust Award

1969
British Council Award

Collections

Tate Collection, London; The Arts Council London; The British Museum, London; Manchester City Art Gallery; Deutsche Bank, London; Slaughter and May; Barclays Art Collection; Private collections

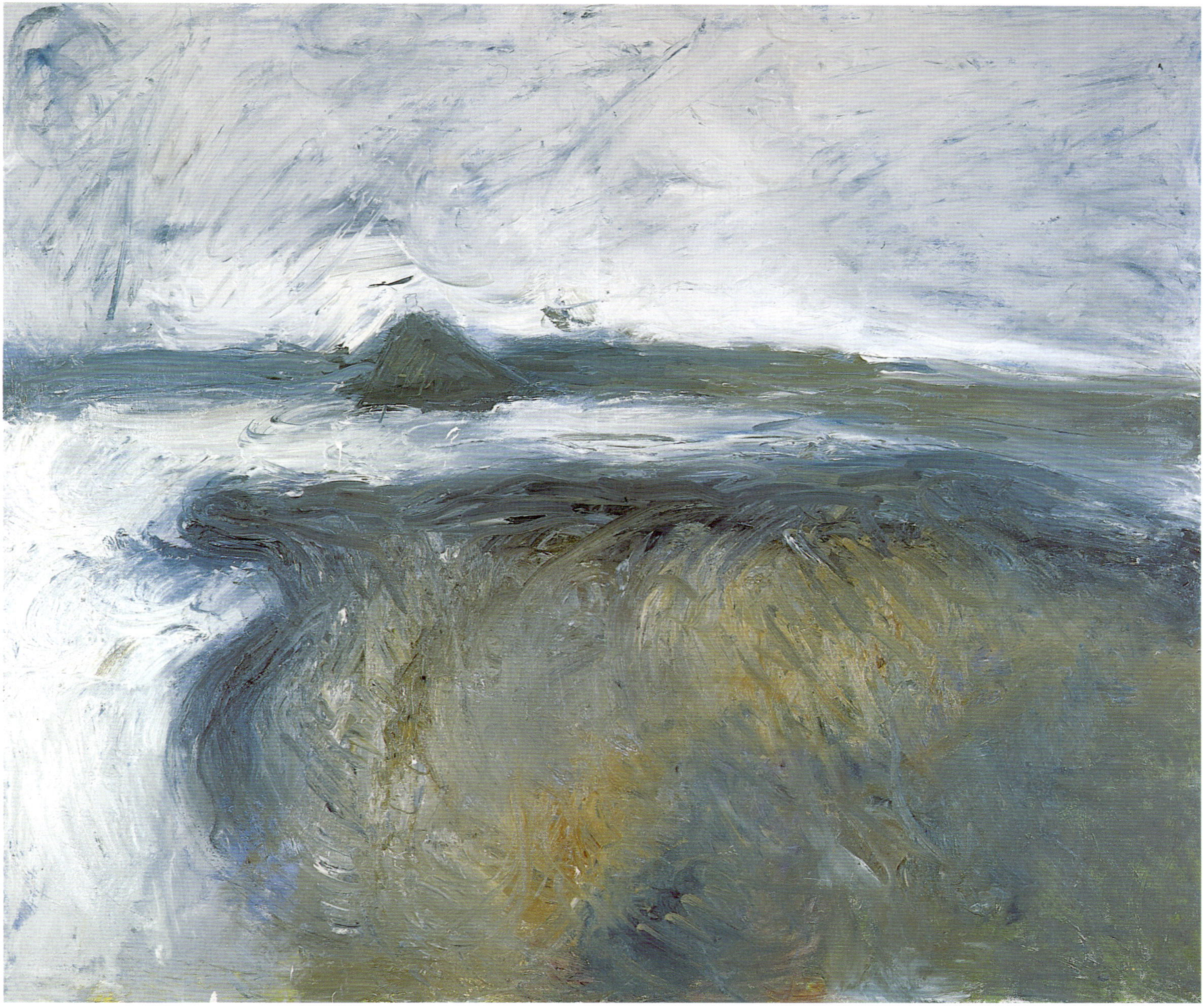

Boat Cove 2006, 152.4 x 182.8 cm, Oil on canvas © the Artist

Mark Surridge

In Britain we have a particular relationship with the landscape, feeling we have an affinity with the natural world and that it forms an aspect of our identity. As a nation we are passionate and protective about it. We have a tendency to idealise it and are comfortable with seeing the landscape as metaphor for states of mind, or as an idyll, a source for poetry and literary visions as well as images of the Sublime.

Mark Surridge's paintings have a lyrical and ephemeral quality of light and form that immediately engages the eye. The Cornish landscape and its weather systems is one subject of interest, but this is only a starting point. Surridge studies the landscape not for its own sake as a retrogressive representational source, but sets out to look beyond it to elicit a simplification of form which results in the creation of a painting which lives as an object in its own right.

Surridge revels in the tone, texture and improvisational malleability of paint and carborundum, searching for the principles of emptiness, calm, simplicity and chance in order to establish an inner tension in his compositions.

His arresting and thickly impastoed surfaces are sparsely marked. The simplest marks, loops and lines often offer a catalogue of bravura signs – the scratch, smudge and splotch – in order to explore spaces that suggest often unidentifiable figurative forms in relation to the landscape.

Most of his paintings have the look of abstract structures, an immediate reminder of the Abstract Expressionists' experimentation with form. But then forms and tones sometimes meld together to suggest an aspect of landscape such as light reflecting off a wet surface and nature's detritus as in *Storm Glow* 2004. In this way Surridge's work offers our imagination space to rest as his paintings hover somewhere between abstraction and figuration.

Selected Biography

1963
Born London.

1981–4
Maidstone College of Art

Selected Solo Exhibitions

2006
Air Voices New Millennium Gallery, St Ives

2005
Elemental Secrets Beardsmore Gallery, London

2004
Weather Changes New Millennium Gallery, St Ives

2003
Land Veils Beardsmore Gallery, London.

2001
Elemental Landscapes New Millennium Gallery, St Ives

Selected Group Exhibitions

2006
London Art Fair 2006, Beardsmore Gallery, London
Critic's Choice (Joseph Clarke) Goldfish Contemporary Fine Art, Penzance

2005
London Art Fair 2005, Beardsmore Gallery, London
Hunting Art Prizes, Royal College of Art, London
Royal Academy Summer Exhibition, London
Critic's Choice (Prof Norbert Lynton), Lemon Street Gallery, Truro
NSA Christmas Exhibition, Campden Gallery, Gloucestershire

2004
Critic's Choice (John Russell Taylor), Newlyn Art Gallery, Newlyn

2003
Glyndebourne Festival Opera, Glyndebourne Gallery, East Sussex
Critic's Choice (Joan Bakewell), Newlyn Art Gallery, Newlyn
Royal Academy Summer Exhibition, London
Weather Report II Newlyn Art Gallery, Newlyn

2002
The Space Between Merriscourt Gallery, Oxfordshire
Ten Beardsmore Gallery, London
Royal Academy Summer Exhibition, London
20/21 British Art Fair, the Commonwealth Institute, London

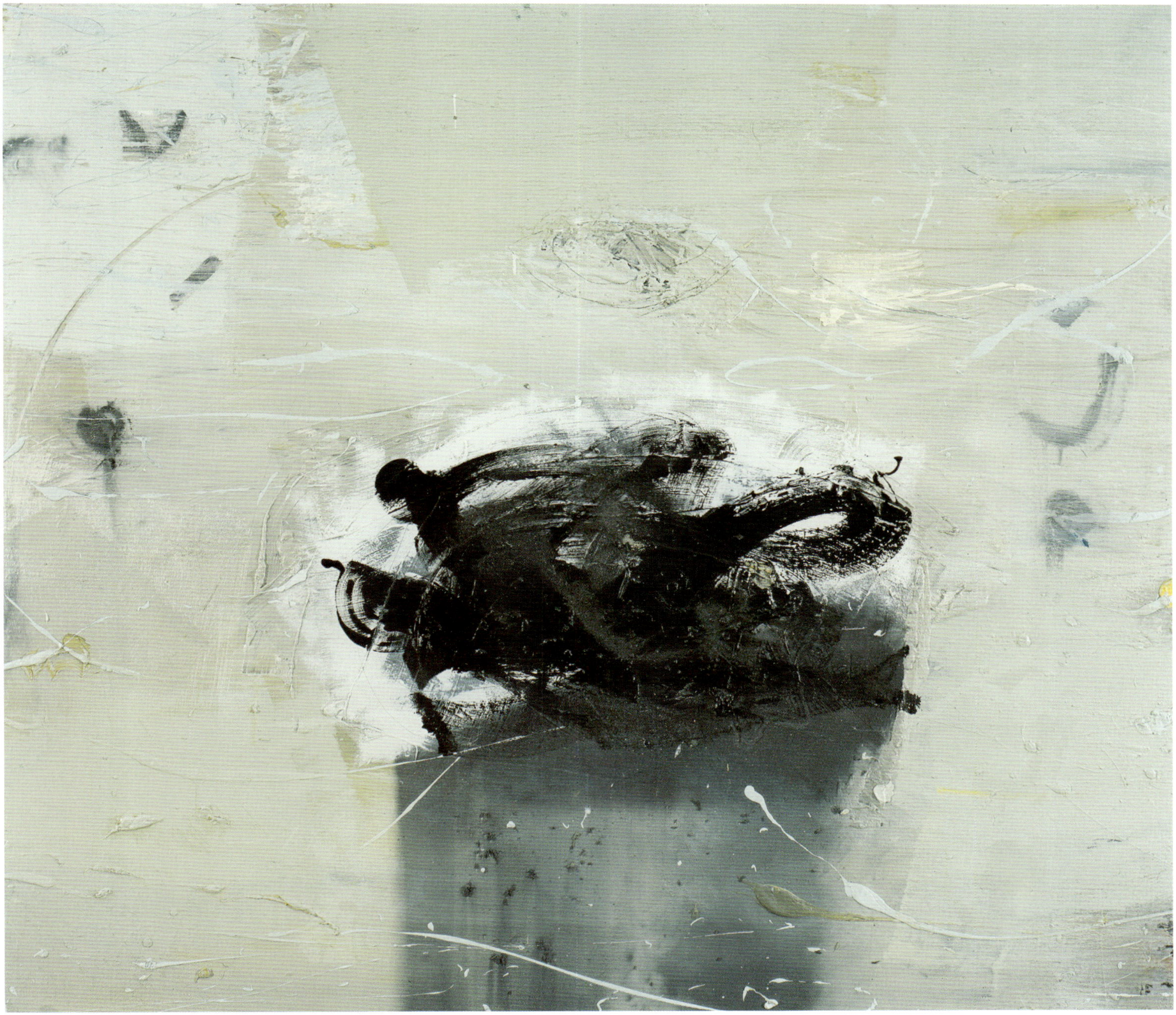

Storm Glow 2004, Oil on canvas, 158 x 182 cm © the Artist

Harriet Bell

Step into the timeless white rooms where Harriet Bell arranges her thoughts and collections of ephemera and objects. See light as a palpable substance entering the purity of the white-washed byre where her ideas reside. Note the poignant remnants of life arranged in grouped fragments – how like a sculptor to 'read' and reflect on the material qualities and similarity of things seen. Try (if you can) not to reflect too much on certain objects which seem to resonate with the more private emotional worlds we carry within us at all times. Try to control the flood of associations that rush into the mind and do not attempt to cede all sense of current reality in this place.

Narrative abounds here. This artist is however, not given to telling but suggesting or hinting and letting us construct our own story. Why are several dolls placed so precisely against her studio wall and floor where they can simultaneously disturb and comfort the psyche? What is the artistic or cultural reference for the group of black wax totemic forms that lie inert and rather menacingly like a new form or type of weapon? These potent fragments act as if they might be great tears in the world, where we might (unwillingly perhaps) be pulled through to a vast space – a parallel world – of our inner thoughts. It is as if, while we were thinking, the world had turned fractionally and set us down in a place where we are in a different relation to it than we were before.

Harriet Bell has lived and worked in Cornwall since 1996, but has carried her sensibility with her across a number of oceans and several cultures. If we were to charge her with the task of gathering ephemera from a square metre of sand, I am certain Bell would return with the minutest of fragments that would have a totally different aesthetic because no-one else had noticed them. The ability to notice things in the interstices of the day-to-day, is the hallmark of a poet-artist. That her objects and texts resonate in the memory with such poignancy is testament to the quality of her noticing.

Selected Biography

1950
Born Ankara, Turkey

1968–9
Studied at the Academie Charpentier, Paris

1969–70
Birmingham College of Art

1973
Graduated Hornsey College of Art

Selected Solo Exhibitions

2006
New Millenium Gallery, St Ives

2002
Newlyn Art Gallery, Newlyn
Keleia Foundation, Gallerija Keleia, Celje, Slovenia

2000
New Millenium Gallery, St Ives

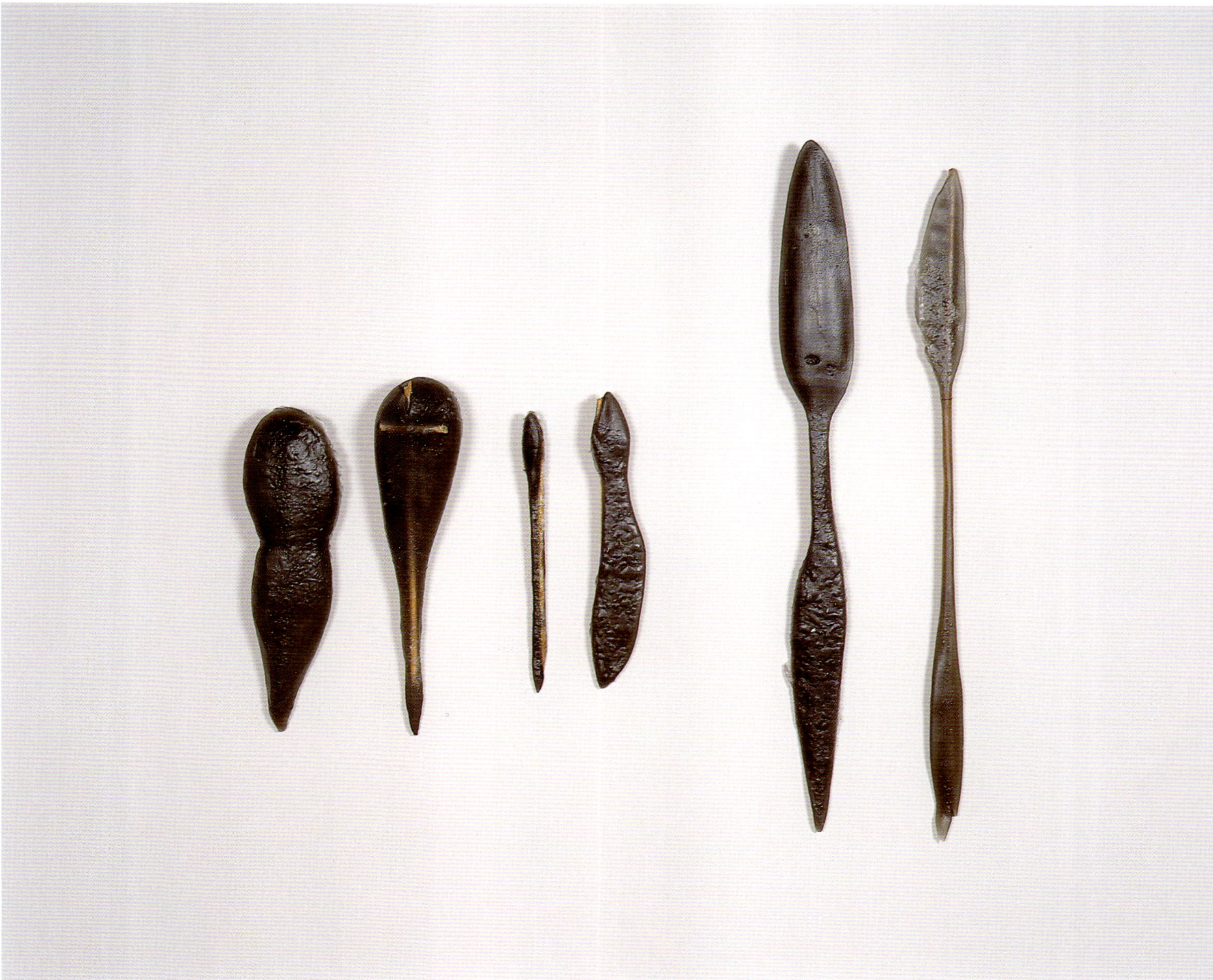

Six Black Objects 2005, Wood and wax, Overall dimensions 52 x 70 x 6 cm © the Artist

Naomi Frears

In her monochromatic paintings of figures lost in thought in an internal landscape, the lightness and open-endedness conventionally associated with drawing (as opposed to painting) is evident. For Naomi Frears, the intuitive journey of making involves repeatedly 'burying' an emerging image under a new surface of paint if it does not have the necessary sense of 'rightness' that she is looking for. Consequently, some paintings may have numerous versions beneath the surface we see.

Frears trained in printmaking, and something of its processes creep in as she works and reworks paintings to arrive at a surface that reveals traces of its making. The painting is hovering in a space that is animated by ghostly remains, giving it an atmosphere and an energy that would not occur if it were completed with flat areas of paint. It seems important to her to make paintings in this way, as if the final visual statement has to be hard-won and that she had to fight the painting's personality as it emerged to achieve a finished result.

What does the term an internal landscape mean? A concept perhaps, which relates to memory and free association of images in relation to the imagination and our inner life. It is noticeable in these paintings that have the vivacity of drawings or prints, every character portrayed looks downwards, averting our gaze. In this way we do not read them as a portrait might be considered, but as a symbolic image for humanity and the peace or melancholia that occupies their thoughts. It is almost as if the figures dream into being what surrounds them. In some instances, the focus on the head is closer and the form is filled with the patterning of a late nineteenth century material. *Wish you were here 2006* renders a white figure with outstretched arms in a supplicatory gesture. The form is set on a black pictorial ground as opposed to white and shadows appear to surround it, setting up more questions for us to intuit.

While painting seems uniquely fit for the purpose of representing the visible world, it might be fair to say that poetry works with the invisible, within the realm of ideas and feeling. Through seeking her own point of perfection in her paintings, Frears is still evolving her language.

Selected Biography

1963
Born Leicestershire

1982–6
BA (Hons) and Printmaking Prize, Sunderland College of Art

1981–2
Foundation, Loughborough College of Art

Selected Solo Exhibitions

2003, 2005, 2007
New Millennium Gallery, St Ives

Selected Group Exhibitions

2006
NSA exhibition, Goldfish Contemporary Fine Art, Penzance
Artists from the Porthmeor Studios, St Ives Society of Artists
From the Edge Sherborne House, Dorset
Porthmeor Printmakers Show, Tate St Ives

2005
3 person show, Newlyn Art Gallery, Newlyn

2004
Critic's Choice (John Russell Taylor), Newlyn Art Gallery, Newlyn
Art London and Lighter Brighter Oliver Contemporary, London
Porthmeor Belgrave Gallery, St Ives
New Cornish Art Edgar Modern, Bath
Drawing? Newlyn Art Gallery, Newlyn

2003
Critic's Choice (Joan Bakewell) Newlyn Art Gallery, Newlyn
Conflict and Resolution Harbour House Gallery, Devon
ID Newlyn Art Gallery, Newlyn

Collections

Falmouth College of Art; Sunderland University; Cornwall County Council; Royal Cornwall Museum, Truro; Slaughter and May, London; Truro School; Private collections

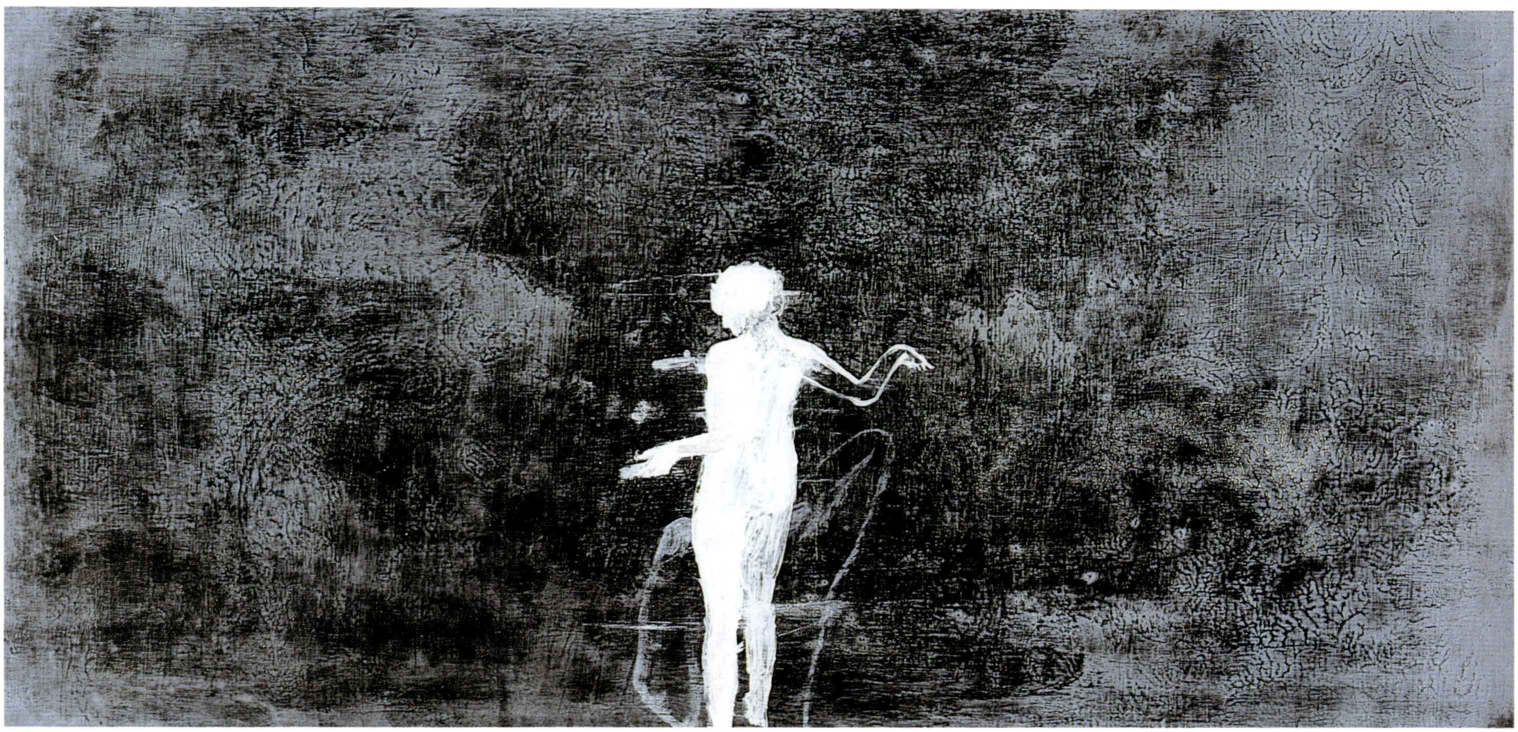

Wish you were here 2006, Acrylic on board, 25 x 51 cm © the Artist

Partou Zia

Partou Zia is an artist whose paintings have always been informed by her surroundings. Iranian by birth and with a sensibility influenced by the icons of that culture, in particular exquisitely illustrated manuscripts, historical paintings and the traditional forms used in Persian textiles, she has lived and worked in Cornwall since 1993. As a poet-painter who works intuitively to keep her paintings open to chance and coincidence, her subject matter has moved between interiors, the still life and – more recently – a narrative exploring love and death through lovers' experiencing happiness, fear and tenderness in their lives. Highly skilful in the manipulation of the material qualities of paint, her subtle tones and gentle colour also echo the ancient landscapes of Cornwall and Wales.

In the past year she has concentrated on a series of self-portraits which present a potent image of female heroism within a landscape that is a synthesis of time, memory, thoughts and visions.

In previous paintings the artist was surrounded by material objects of symbolic importance such as books, gloves and vessels. In this new series of paintings she is presented in the context of a wilder nature – a landscape covered with a mere skin of green and trees which have a metaphysical presence. The burning bush is a symbol of regeneration whereby God spoke to Moses via a conflagration that did not destroy the bush. This is a symbolic representation of the greater realm beyond that which we know and understand where the artist-heroine is making a direct emotional communication with us, her observers.

Selected Biography

1958
Born Tehran, Persia

1970
Emigrated to England

1977–80
BA (Hons) History of Art, University of Warwick

1986–91
BA (Hons) Fine Art, Slade School of Fine Art

1993
Moved to Cornwall

1998–2001
Falmouth College of Arts and University of Plymouth, PhD

Selected Solo Exhibitions

2005
The Grey Syllable Art First, London

2004
Thought Paintings Art First, London

2003
Entering the Visionary Zone Tate St Ives

2002, 2000
Art Space Gallery, London
Plymouth Art Centre

1998
Newlyn Art Gallery, Newlyn

Selected Group Exhibitions

2006
Translations Art First, London

2004
Spoilt for Choice A Christmas Show Art First, London

1998
In/Sight Exeter University

1996
Landscapes from Penwith Hastings Museum and Gallery

1995
John Moores Exhibition 19, Walker Art Gallery, Liverpool

1990
Works on Paper The Boundary Gallery, London

1989
Young Contemporaries Whitworth Gallery, Manchester

Awards and Residencies

2005, 2003, 2001
Arts Council England, South West

2003
Tate St Ives Artist in Residence

Collections

British Museum, London; Private collections

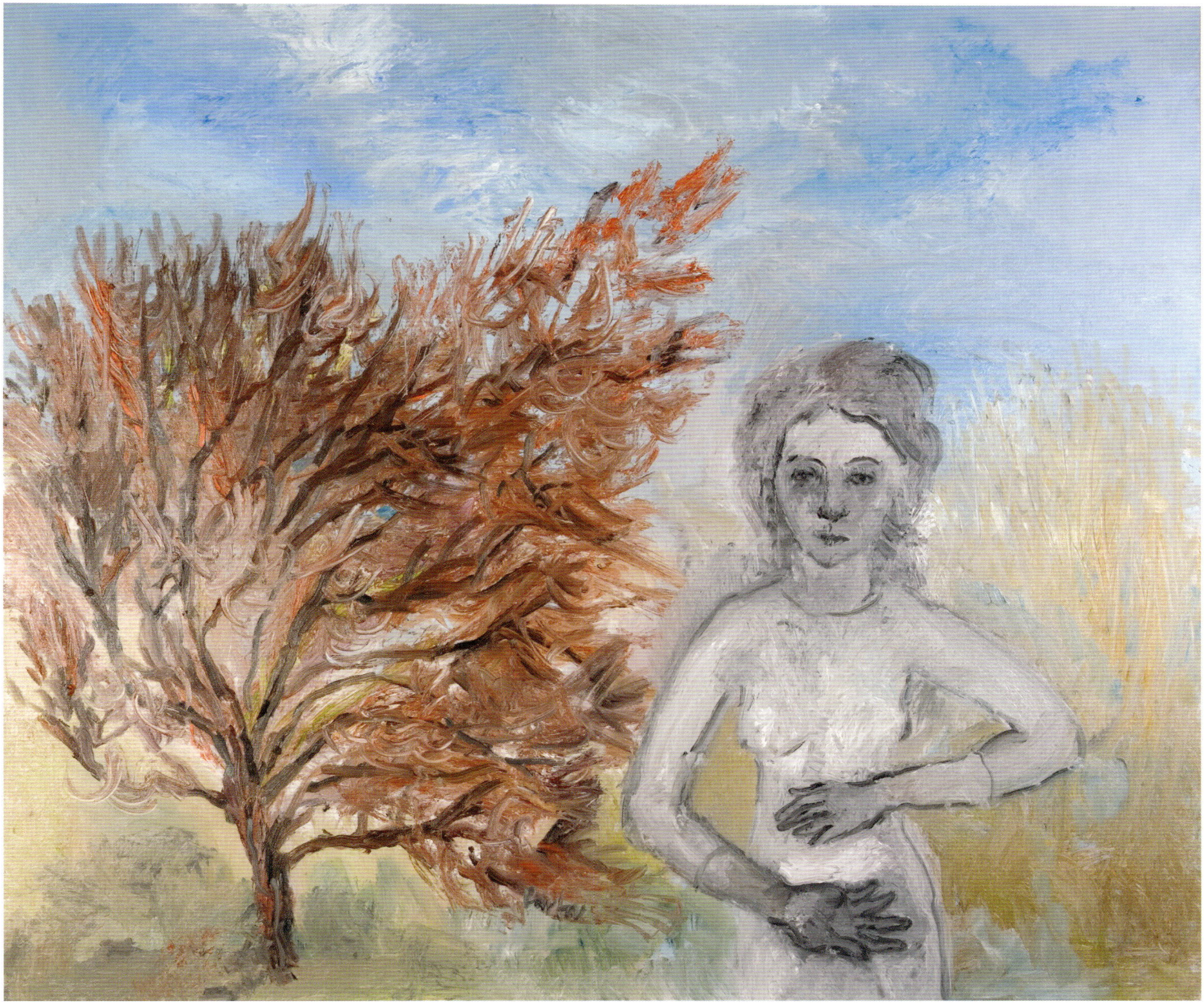

The Burning Bush 2006, Oil on canvas, 152 x 183 cm, Private collection © the Artist

Lucy Willow

Lucy Willow is drawn repeatedly to questions and ideas that reflect love, loss and the profound level of beauty that can be sourced from them. She is fascinated by the poetry of certain materials such as house and marble dust, both of which link with her thoughts on memory and history. This new work *Celestial Dust Rug* 2007 comes from a series of prayer rugs that explore ideas relating to the impermanence of everything in life.

The rugs have been made in response to particular environments and derive from a piece *Dust Rug* 2003: an ornate carpet made with household dust for a domestic setting. The artist became interested in using dust to create traditional prayer rugs which reflect on the fragility and often futility of prayer. Recent prayer rugs have been made in white marble dust, the first in the series using elements from Hieronymus Bosch's painting *The Garden of Earthly Delights* 2004 for the centre instead of the traditional symbol of Heaven. The subversion of the traditional meanings within a prayer rug is played with to give a new meaning.

The rugs are made directly onto the surface of the floor by sieving the dust through a stencil made in fine netting fabric. They are context specific and exist only for the duration of the exhibition. They are fragile and fine and could at any moment be disturbed if blown or touched. Each rug is swept away at the end of the exhibition; nothing is forever, apart from our memories. Willow is interested in the idea that impermanence is the essence of everything and she has used the material of dust as a vehicle in which to explore this concept and make visible otherwise intangible ideas.

Selected Biography

1967
Born Whitstable, Kent

2000–3
BA (Hons), Fine Art (First Class), Falmouth College of Art, Cornwall

1995–7
Foundation in Art and Design, Falmouth College of Art, Cornwall

1987–9
Diploma, Graphic Design, Canterbury College of Art, Kent

Selected Group Exhibitions

2006
Art in Hotels Brighton Fringe Festival
Make it real Whitstable, Kent

2005
Transition 6 Newlyn Art Gallery, Newlyn
Art in Romney Marsh, 2005

2004
Smithfield Abattoir, *Wrestling With Angels*, London
Taxi Gallery, Cambridge

2002
FIDEM, Monnaie de Paris
Royal Academy Summer Exhibition

2001
Cork Vision Centre, Cork
Oriel Henry Thomas Gallery, Camarthen

Selected Awards

2006
Arts Council England Award (In-transit, mobile art project)

2005
Unltd, Millennium Award (In-transit, mobile project)

2001
BAMS (British Art Medal Society) student award, First Prize
Art For All Awards, Lottery Grant (Penwith Artists Led Projects)

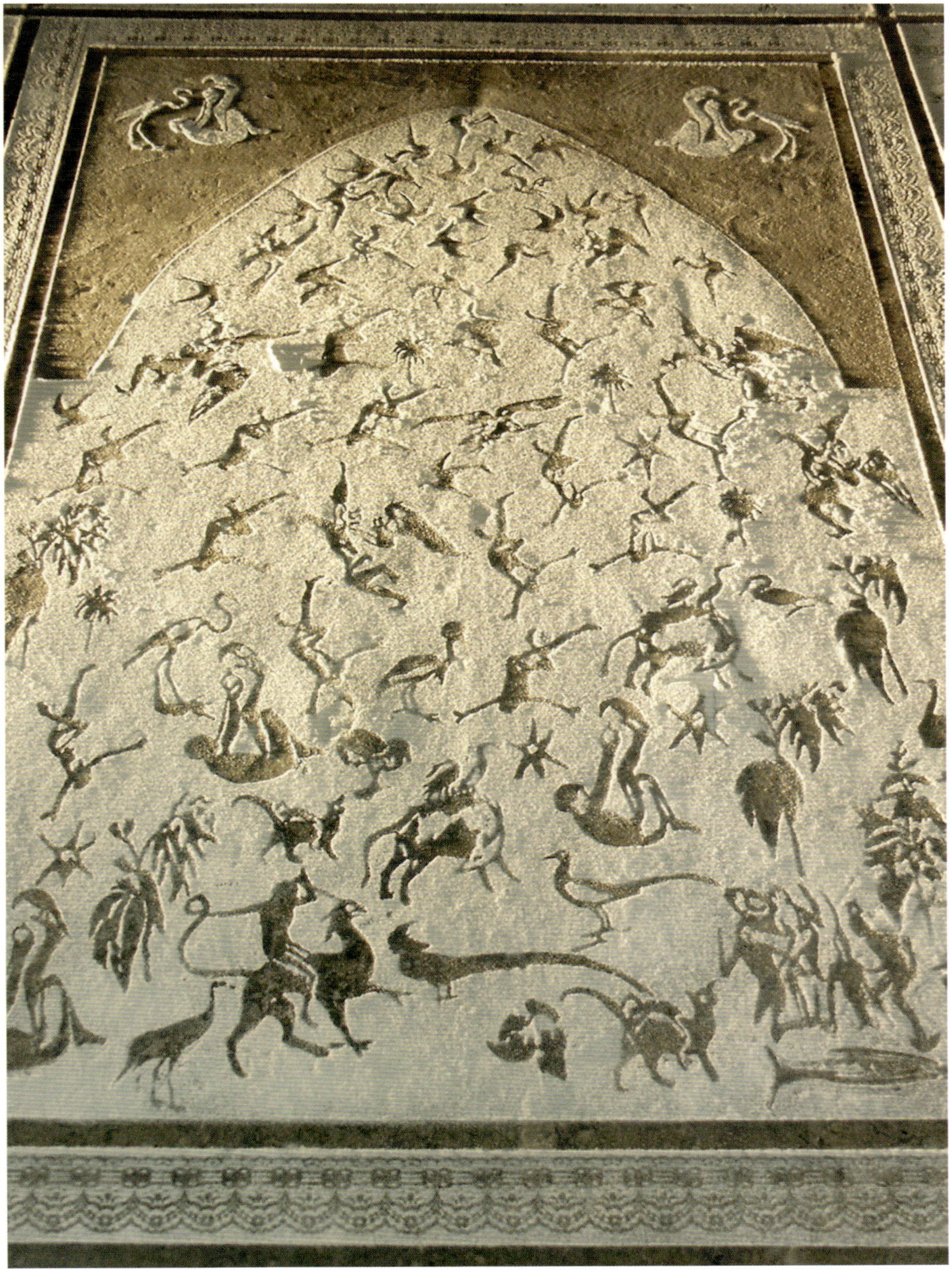

Marble Dust Rug 2004, White marble dust, 38.1 x 25.4 cm © the Artist

Philip Medley

Philip Medley evokes the mutability of material in his sculpture *Easy it is for a God* 2004, through the process of cutting, carving and welding of sheet steel – an industrially manufactured material – which is then protected from the elements with a 'skin' of paint. This helps to unify the form so that the viewer can engage with the immediacy of its physicality and the enigma of its character, without being distracted by the many details which make up the whole.

Although, as the title denotes, the work initially appropriates iconography and stylised landscapes of European medieval painting, this sculpture synthesises many disparate elements, paraphrasing and contrasting, hiding and revealing. Medley sets out to allow his sculptures to evolve naturally and without contrivance to achieve a fully independent and evocative presence. The gradual process of transformation – depending from which vantage point the eye falls – finds expression in the sculpture as a passage from one form to another. In this way, the narrative within the sculptural form is given up slowly as if the sculpture had a number of different guises or personalities.

Sculptures that are formed by the stacking of material often provide us with an opportunity to experience the very substance of it in a primary constructive form. In this instance we are denied the experience of steel as material. And what we know from experience to be solid and hard appears to us as soft and sensual, charmed into the appearance of other materials like clay or rubber.

Looking at works that are layered or constructed vertically, creates a strong relationship with our bodies. They also provoke a feeling of travelling in a foreign medium or of being able to see some hidden aspect of the object as our eye roams in, up, across and around its surface. Questions of what can possibly be representational start to arise in our minds. Although steel is tough, with a painted surface – a skin of plastic – the structure of this 'skin' envelops the form and not only unites different formal elements but also marks a boundary between the inside and the outside of the work.

Medley asserts that the best sculpture demands re-examination. It leads the eye; it forces you to think as well as to feel. It elicits questions and contradictions but through its malleability allows physical intimacy combined with monumentality. Its maturity gives the audience information – but not too much. The complexities within the sculptures reflect a human nature.

Selected Biography

1962
Born Chester

Solo Exhibitions

2003
Selected prints and sculptures, New Art Centre Sculpture Park and Gallery, Wiltshire

Selected Group Exhibitions

2006
Broomhill, Devon: Paintings and Sculptures

2003–6
The Sculpture Park, Surrey

2000
Sculpture in the Square Mile, London

1999–2006
Royal Academy of Art Summer Exhibition

1993–2006
New Art Centre Sculpture Park, Wiltshire

1998
Late 20th Century Sculpture Millfield

1993
Young Sculptors New Art Centre Gallery, London
15 Sculptors Riverdale Sculpture Park, London

1990
Seven Sculptors Oxford Arts Festival

1989
Ardingly Sculpture Project, Sussex

1988–92
Whitechapel Open Exhibition, London

1986–8
Sculpture at the Herbert Read Gallery, Canterbury 1986–8

Awards

1994
Pollock Krasner Foundation, New York

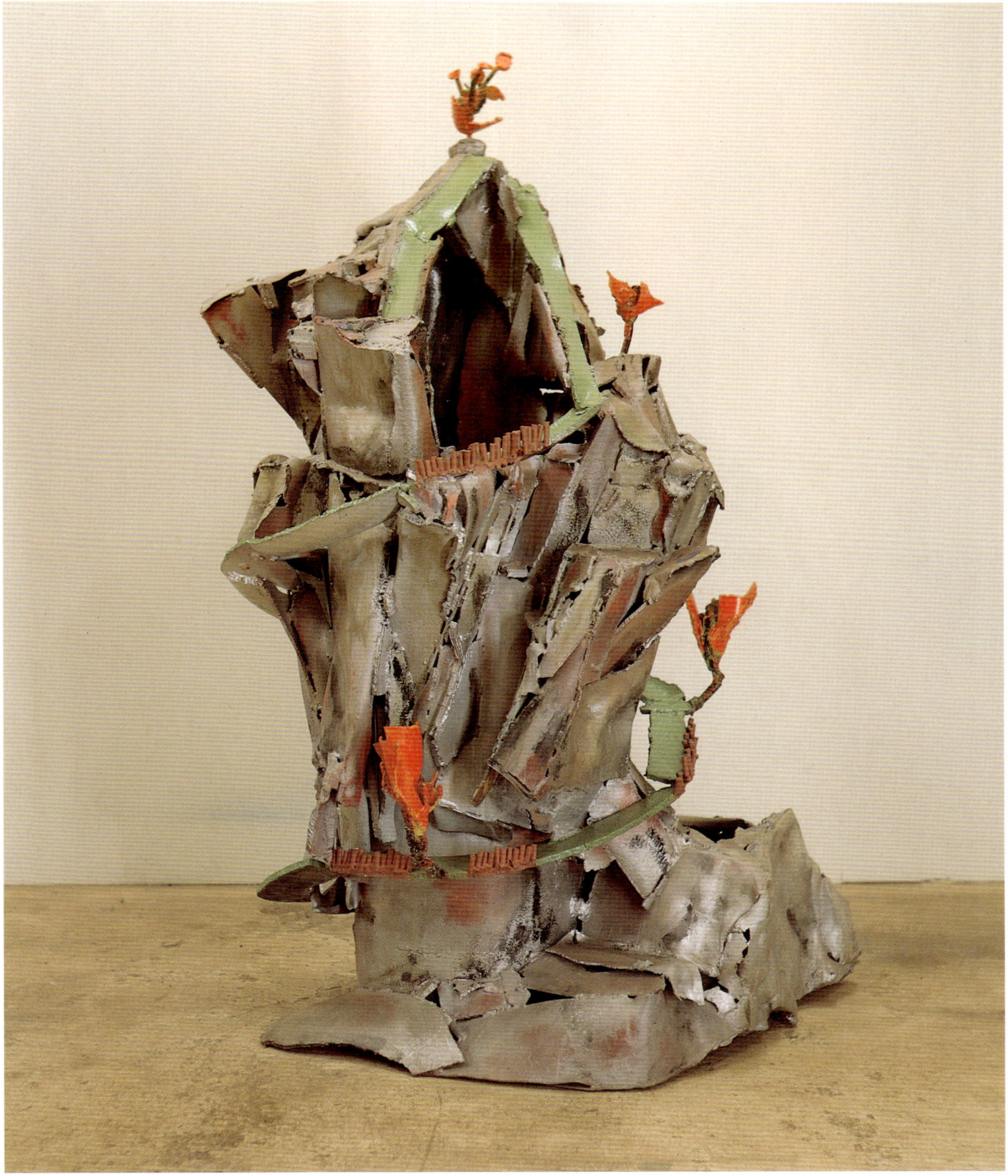

Calvary 2003, Steel, 194 x 131 x 146 cm © the Artist

Lisa Wright

Since coming to live in Cornwall in the mid 1990s, Lisa Wright has been exploring the depiction of children – using her family as a source – to realise a rigorous body of figurative paintings. Trained in the classic tradition at the Royal Academy Schools, she is grounded in the daily discipline of drawing and emotional engagement with her subject.

In her recent expressive paintings of children portrayed against a heightened version of nature at night, it is possible to experience a new sense of space. This is created by the painting as its flat areas of colour seem to expand beyond the canvas to fill architectural space. Wright luxuriates in the colour, texture and fluidity of her medium. Inscribing the paintings' surfaces and using her brush as a drawing instrument, she heightens this energetic contrast with more thickly painted and textured areas.

Her landscape references are a synthesis of a number of factors which allow her to play with subject, form, colour and space to create works of great theatre and poignancy. Night photography and the glamorous saturated colour that results from its technology, together with remembered atmospheres, supernaturally changed places and lighting effects, are several ingredients in the mix. The landscape surrounding her home at Crelly in Cornwall is subject to localised mists sometimes resulting in 'white-out' conditions affording her the opportunity to think about nature in monochromatic contrasts such as dark forms against light backgrounds and their reverse.

On close examination of the painting *Shadow Branches* 2006 it is hard not to also be reminded of the British artist Mark Wallinger's tender sculpture *Ecce Homo* which draws inspiration from the artistic tradition of portraying humanity as Christ, the bearer of our sorrows.

Selected Biography

1965
Born Kent

1990–3
MA Painting,
Royal Academy Schools, London

1984–7
BA (Hons),
Maidstone College of Art

Solo Exhibitions

2006
Lemon Street Gallery, Truro

2005
Beach Paintings Beardsmore Gallery, London

2003
Pool Paintings Beardsmore Gallery, London
Lemon Street Gallery, Truro

2001
Beardsmore Gallery, London

Selected Group Exhibitions

2006
The Sovereign European Art prize, London
Royal Academy Summer Exhibition, London
To the Edge Beardsmore Gallery, London
NSA Summer Exhibition, Goldfish Contemporary Fine Art, Penzance

2005
Critic's Choice (Norbert Lynton), NSA

2003–5
Lemon Street Gallery, Truro
25th Anniversary Hunting Art Prizes, London
Royal Academy Summer Exhibition, London
Art London Beardsmore Gallery, London
Invited artist, Hunting Art Prizes, London

2003
Hunting Art Prizes, Royal College of Art, London (first prize)
Critic's Choice (Joan Bakewell), Newlyn Art Gallery, Newlyn

Selected Awards and Prizes

2005
25th Anniversary Most Popular Painting Prize at Hunting Art Prizes
Shortlisted for the Sovereign European Art Prize

2003
Hunting Art Prizes, first prize
Arts Council of England Award

1993
The Royal Overseas League Travel Scholarship

1992
The Royal Academy Premiums Painting Prize

Collections

Guinness Collection; Unilever; BUPA; Zeneca; Private collections

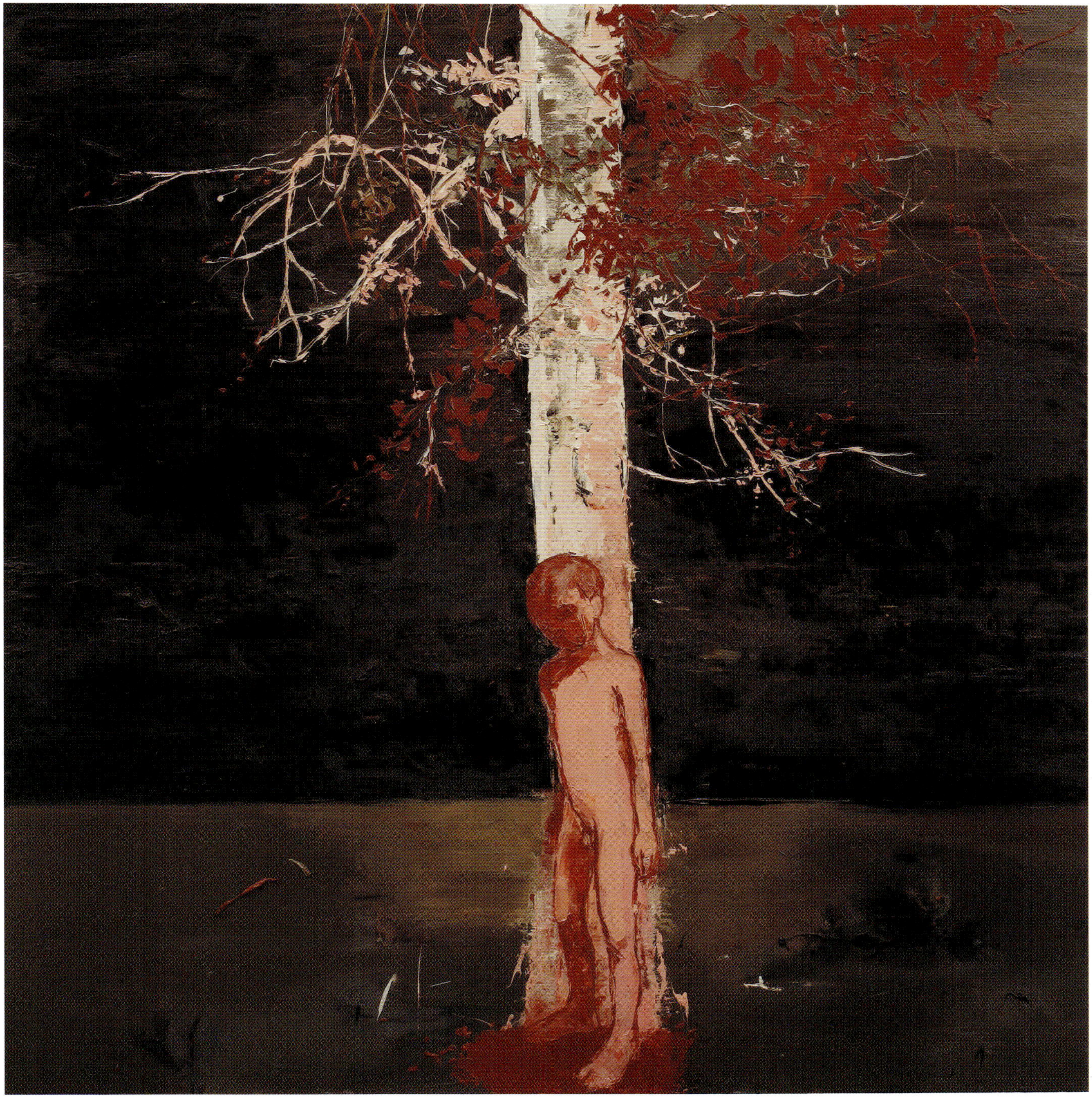

Shadow Branches 2006, Oil on canvas, 152.5 x 152.5 cm © the Artist

Delpha Hudson

Delpha Hudson uses performance and video in her work, which focuses on the idea of re-representing 'female'. Hudson is interested in the potential dialogue that may ensue through the interplay between performance, video, documentation and archive material.

Her context-specific performances have been presented in a variety of public places including streets, shopping arcades and shop windows where there is a dialogue and interaction with an audience beyond the convention of the gallery. Her video work is often combined with performance where she explores her experience as a designated female and mother. Much of her work examines feminism, particularly in relation to women and the objects they value.

In *Miss-Readings* 2007, Hudson will be playing with visitors' expectations and context of the historically and politically correct museum tour. In performing an alternative tour at the Barbara Hepworth Museum in St Ives, the artist engages with various sites; Hepworth the person, her role as an artist, the place where she lived and worked from 1949 until 1975, moving on to consider Hepworth the history and Hepworth the museum. As a critical intervention that aims to strip away public expectation of hushed formality in a museum space that was the artist's home, the performance is not critical of Hepworth, but highlights the importance of her place in art history.

Through this context-specific performance, the artist hopes to engage directly with the public in personal and textual exchanges. These may be banal, esoteric, slightly irreverent and possibly absurd but will draw out issues of Hepworth mythologies, theories about her sculpture and historical materialism. In playing with the persona and performance of the museum guide, Hudson will engage the public in new conversations and possibilities of site and history.

Selected Biography

1963
Born Surrey

1985
BA (Hons) History,
University of London

2001
BA (Hons) Fine Art,
Coventry University

2003
MA Visual Performance,
Dartington College of Art

Selected Solo and Group Exhibitions

2006
1,000 Kisses, site-specific performance,
The Window Gallery, Birmingham

2005
Pleasure in Slowness, site-specific performance at Mailbox Intervention Festival, Birmingham

Lecture on site-specificity for BAIT, ALIAS funded series of seminars

Comfort Zones, digital photographs and video, Wolverhampton University

2004
Performance lecture, *A Body of Work*, Coventry University.

Something's Fishy, performance, Surface Gallery, Nottingham

Dos Palabras, performance and video for *Stringing a Sentence Together*, at the Tabernacle, Notting Hill, London

On The margin, performance video shown at Tulca, Ireland, Nov 2005, Body Parts Festival (SSA), Edinburgh, Jan 2005, *Performance in Nature*, Serbia, 2004, and the Phoenix, Exeter Sept 2004

Dead Women Walking, a quasi-historical walking performance, Part of *Art, what is it good for?* Curated by Tracey Warr

Tealady, street action at SEEN Festival Leicester.

2003
Inte(xt)change, street action at Exeter HEM festival

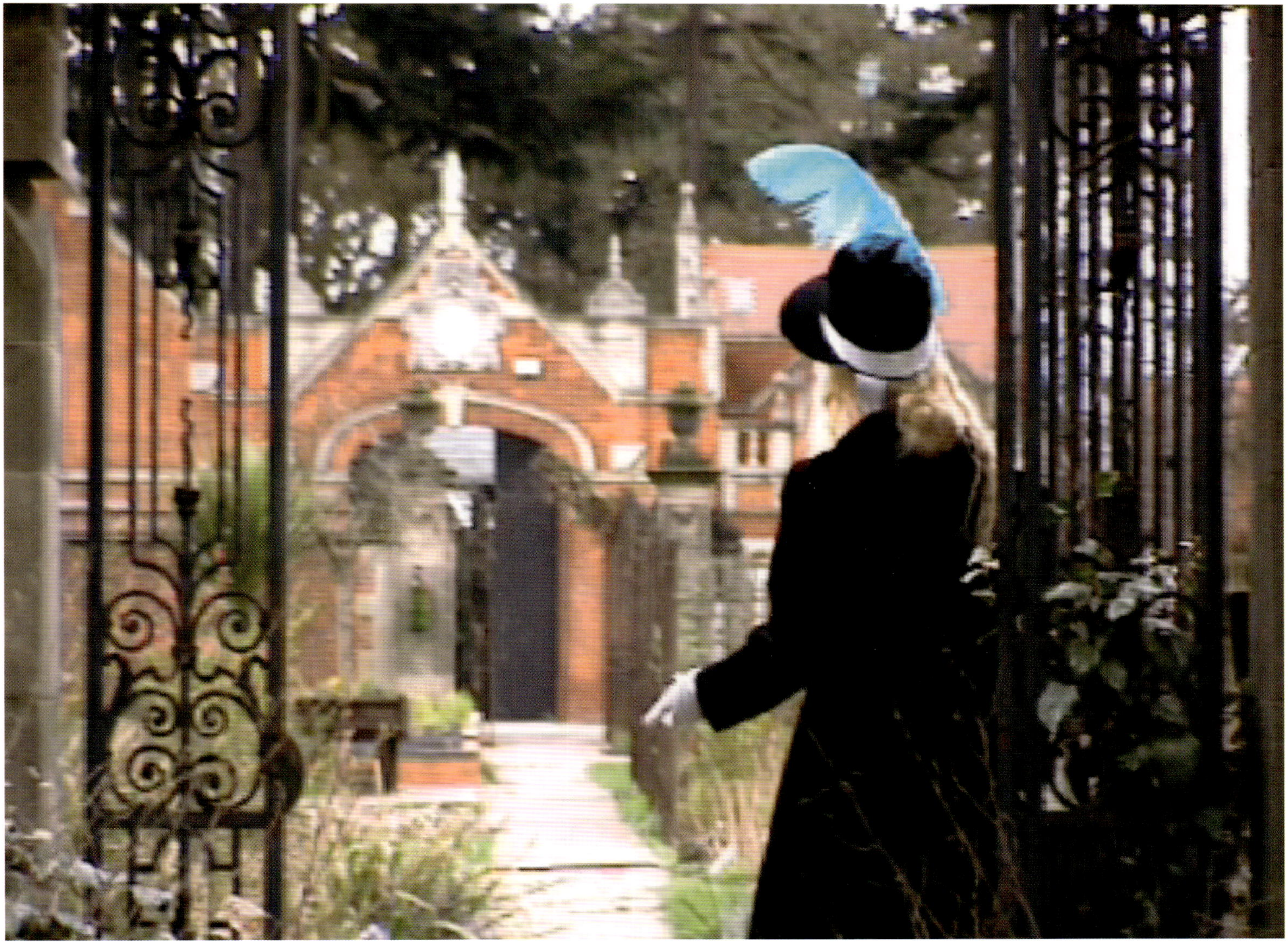

A Walk with Jane Austen 2000, Performance, Blossomfield House © the Artist

Cathy Watkins

In order to escape the weighty artistic legacy of St Ives and the seductive landscapes of Cornwall, Catharine Watkins has been studying childrens' toys. In particular, females from the Bratz™ series of sexualised dolls, masks of the Overlord, weapons of the Underworld, toys produced with a theme for Halloween and the ubiquitous Barbie™. Based in St Ives and Penzance, Watkins finds a plethora of subjects to study, draw and paint, in the two local Woolworth stores. Barbie is an 'icon' and powerful presence in her personal childhood and is remembered as an object of compelling desirability. Barbie also happens to be one of the most successful brands of the twentieth century.

For Watkins, Barbie represents much of what is most damaging (and misogynistic) in our culture, particularly regarding the representation of the female form. Barbie's anatomy bears no relation to any female at any age and worse still, she plays a large part in the extreme sexualisation of children's toys and the extent to which current notions of 'beauty' are established in relation to the influences of pornography. In the artist's attempts to represent her she quickly discovered that she is not only incapable of standing unaided (her feet are at an angle in order to fit her into high-heeled shoes), she is also unable to sit without her legs open. Her most stable position is either on all fours with her ass in the air or attached by a wire to her plinth.

In *Head First* 2006 Watkins is playing on the originality and power of a cultural brand image as well as pondering the post modern status of American culture (from where Barbie originates). In choosing to paint Barbie, she has realised the medium's unique potential to fashion a new version of reality without the need for props. In her fantasy world Barbie is not a heroic protagonist occupying a canvas in the convention of painting (or in the mind of an eight year old). Instead she is portrayed in her most stable position, almost incidentally and as much of an accidental occurrence as are the splodges, paint rings and other paint remnants which appear on the cardboard on which she is represented.

Selected Biography

1963
Born Portsmouth, Hampshire

1979–81
Portsmouth College of Art

1981–4
BA Fine Art,
Goldsmiths College of Art

2002
Moved to Cornwall

2006
Currently studying University College Falmouth, MA 20th Century Art and Design

Selected Solo Exhibitions

2005
Postcards from St Ives, The Gallery in Cork Street, London

2003
Coast to coast, The Gallery in Cork Street, London

2001
Beside the Sea, The Gallery in Cork Street, London

1999
Painting holiday, The Conningsby Gallery, London

1992
Intimate distance, The Photographer's Gallery, London

Selected Group Exhibitions

2005
The Little Picture Show, Rainy Day Gallery, Penzance
Artaid 2005, Royal College of Art, London
Treemendous, Falmouth Art Gallery, Falmouth

2004
The Little Picture Show, Rainy Day Gallery, Penzance

2003
Women at Charles Russell, New Fetter Lane, London

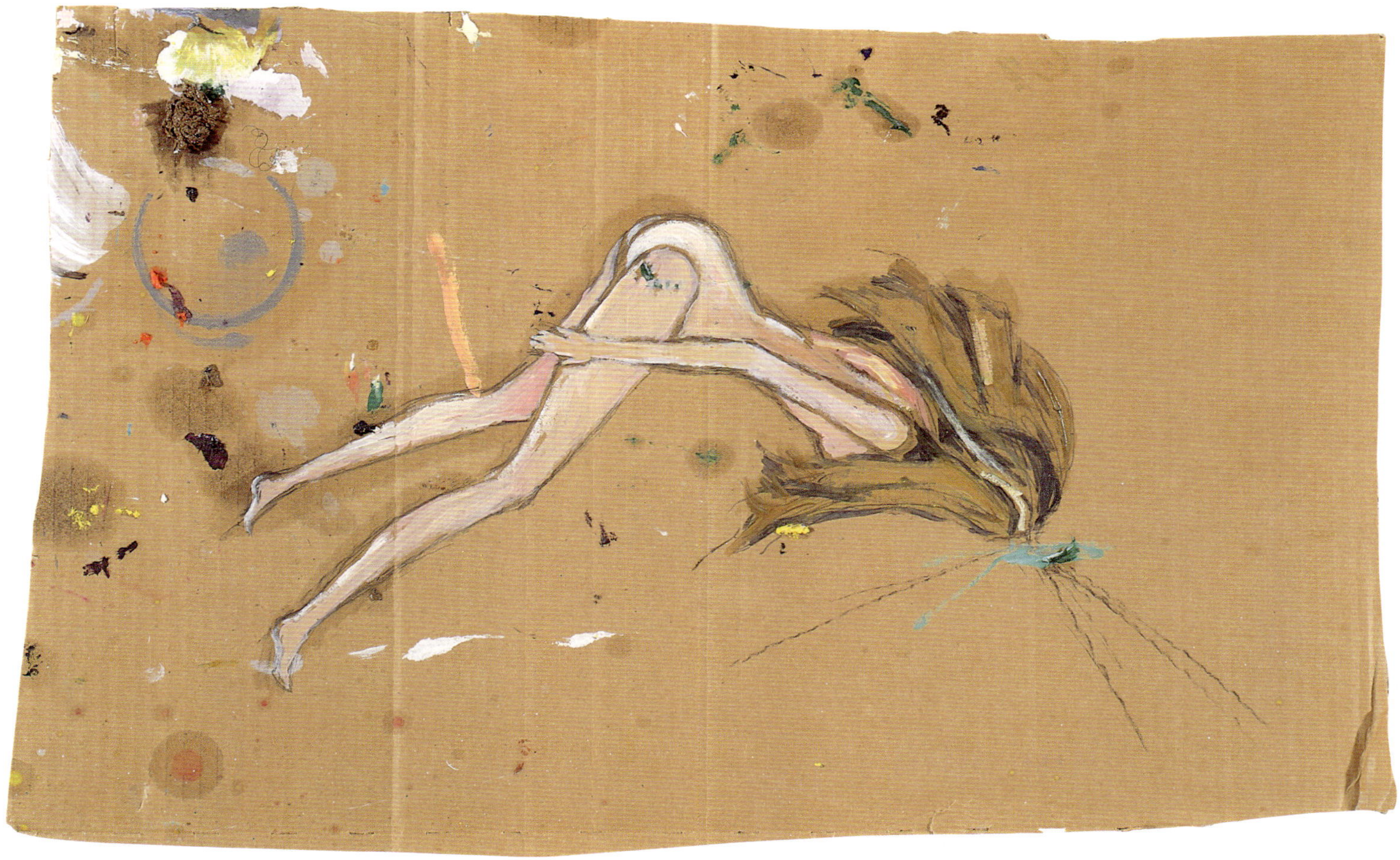

Head First 2006, Charcoal and oil paint on cardboard, 33 x 54 cm © the Artist

Exhibition List of Works

Harriet Bell
Cocoon 1998
Earth, ashes, plaster
overall: 70 x 26 x 19 cm
© the Artist

Harriet Bell
Six Black Objects 2005
Wood, wax
Overall dimensions
52 x 70 x 6 cm
© the Artist

Harriet Bell
Untitled 2006
Pencil on paper
image: 62 x 86 cm
© the Artist

Neil Canning
Shine 2006
Oil on canvas
76 x 91 cm
Collection Mr and Mrs A W Wright
© the Artist

Richard Cook
Boat Cove 2006
Oil on canvas
152.4 x 182.8 cm
© the Artist

Jessica Cooper
All the things I should have said but didn't 2006
Acrylic and pencil on canvas
97 x 92 cm
© the Artist

Jessica Cooper
Cast 2006
Acrylic on canvas
83 x 87 cm
© the Artist

Andy Currie
Gillying Dune 2006
Mixed media
23 x 10 cm
© the Artist

Andy Currie
Egg and Spoon Race 2006
Mixed media
25 x 25 x 34 cm
© the Artist

Andy Currie
My Lucky Star is a rubbish Scorpion 2004
Mixed media
23 x 35 x 23 cm
© the Artist

Andy Currie
Ping Pong Fans 2006
Mixed Media
34 x 23 x 23 cm
© the Artist

Andy Currie
Blustery Showers 2004
Mixed Media
180 x 180 x 60 cm
© the Artist

Naomi Frears
Wish you were here 2006
Acrylic on board
25 x 51 cm
© the Artist

Anthony Frost
Surface Noise (when it blows it stacks) 2006
Acrylic and collage on canvas
121.9 x 210.8 cm
© the Artist

Luke Frost
Volts No 7 2006
Acrylic on canvas
152.5 x 152.5 cm
On loan Somerville Gallery, Plymouth
© the Artist

Andy Hughes
Gwithian Beach 2005
Photograph
51 x 51 cm
© the Artist

Andy Hughes
Porthmeor Beach 2005
Photograph
51 x 51 cm
© the Artist

Andy Hughes
Gwithian Beach 2005
Photograph
51 x 51 cm
© the Artist

Delpha Hudson
Miss-Readings 2007
Performance
Dimensions Variable
© the Artist
Commissioned by Tate St Ives for the Barbara Hepworth Museum

Sax Impey
Event 9 2005
Mixed media on wood
204 x 204 cm © the Artist

Matthew Lanyon
Highground III 2006
Oil on canvas
168.9 x 168.9 cm
© the Artist

Jonty Lees
Skimming Stones
2005
Video
© the Artist

Jonty Lees
Skimming Stones 2005
Oil on Linen
41 x 59 cm
© the Artist
Painted by Andrew Palmer

Amanda Lorens
Tango Privado I 2006
Live Art
Dimensions variable
© the Artist

Amanda Lorens
Tango Privado II 2007
Video and audio installation
Dimensions variable
© the Artist

Phil Medley
Easy it is for a God 2004
Painted Steel
205 x 212 x 225 cm
© the Artist

Phil Medley
Calvary 2003
Steel
194 x 131 x 146 cm
© the Artist

Richard Nott
Striation (A) 2005
Mixed media on panel
153 x 153 x 6 cm
© the Artist

Hadrian Pigott
Rifiuti 2005
Video, duration 30 minutes
Dimensions variable
© the Artist
With thanks to Robert Woof
and The Wordsworth Trust

Hadrian Pigott
Natura Morta (Rome, 11 July 2005, 14:21) 2005
Colour print
120 x 80 cm
© the Artist

Michael Porter
Issel Road 2005
Acrylic and oil on canvas
121 x 111 cm
Purdy Hicks Gallery, London
© the Artist

Michael Porter
From the Cornish Stones Series 05-11-04 2006
Photogram and oil paint
35 x 28 cm
Purdy Hicks Gallery, London
© the Artist

Michael Porter
From the Cornish Stones Series 09-11-04 2006
Photogram and oil paint
35 x 28 cm
Purdy Hicks Gallery, London
© the Artist

Ged Quinn
Asleep by the Light of Glow-worms 2005
Oil on linen
183 x 220 cm
Private collection
© the Artist
Courtesy Wilkinson Gallery, London

Iain Robertson
Poet's Love Series II No I 2006
Oil on canvas
90 x 90 cm
© the Artist

Jesse Leroy Smith
Leopard 2006
Oil on canvas
178 x 140 cm
© the Artist

Jesse Leroy Smith
Smoke 2006
Lithograph on paper
75 x 60 cm
© the Artist

Mark Surridge
Storm Glow 2004
Oil on canvas
158 x 182 cm
© the Artist

Cathy Watkins
Head First 2006
Charcoal and oil paint
on cardboard
33 x 54 cm
© the Artist

Andy Whall
In An Atlantic Wave 2006
Video
© the Artist
Site-ations International
Conference 2006, *Sense in Place*,
Model Arts and Niland Gallery,
Sligo, Ireland, June 2006,
previously shown as part of
conference presentation in
collaboration with Dr Chris Short

Lucy Willow
Celestial Dust Rug 2007
Iron spangles, black dust,
carborundum
Dimensions variable
© the Artist

Lisa Wright
Shadow Branches 2006
Oil on canvas
152.5 x 152.5 cm
© the Artist

Lisa Wright
Night Beach 2006
Mixed media on paper
40.4 x 40.4 cm
© the Artist

Clare Wardman
Prima Vista 25 August 2005 (Light Tracking) 2005
Oil on canvas
76 x 91 cm
© the Artist

Partou Zia
The Burning Bush 2006
Oil on canvas
152 x 183 cm
Private collection
© the Artist

Partou Zia
Self I 2006
Pencil on paper
57 x 38.5 cm
© the Artist

Partou Zia
Self II 2006
Pencil on paper
57 x 38.5 cm
© the Artist

Partou Zia
Self III 2006
Pencil on paper
57 x 35.5 cm
© the Artist

Partou Zia
Self IV 2006
Pencil on paper
57 x 38.5 cm
© the Artist

Partou Zia
Self V 2006
Pencil on paper
57 x 38.5 cm
© the Artist

Acknowledgements

It is a pleasure to thank the many artists and colleagues who have responded enthusiastically to requests for information and other help in the preparation of this exhibition. All of the artists in this exhibition have given advice and information on their works as well as biographical details. We are grateful to the artists for making their work available for this important exhibition. Private owners of several works have been extremely generous in lending them. Others have helped us in various ways including; Matthew McDonald, Norman Pollard, Simon Pollard, Dave Davies, Fiona Cattrell, Vicki Stevens, Arwen Fitch, Alex Lambley, Kerry Rice and Susan Lamb and our colleague in London Mary Bustin.

This exhibition has allowed us to meet artists in their workplace and get to know more about their practice. The project has given us a lot of pleasure and satisfaction to put together and we hope that, as a result of our research, similar exhibitions will occur in the future.

First published 2007 by order of the Tate Trustees by Tate St Ives in association with Tate Publishing, a division of Tate Enterprises Ltd, Millbank, London SW1P 4RG
www.tate.org.uk www.tate.org.uk/publishing

On the occasion of the exhibition:
Art Now Cornwall
at Tate St Ives 3 February – 13 May 2007

The exhibition and publication has been supported by:
Tate St Ives Members and Tate Members

British Library Cataloguing in Publication Data:
A catalogue record of this book is available from the British Library
ISBN 978 185 43775 17

Texts by Susan Daniel-McElroy and Sara Hughes
© The authors and Tate 2007
All images courtesy of artists and lenders © as credited
All photograpy © the photographers:
Vince Bevan pages 15, 17, 39, 47, 49;
Simon Cook pages 13, 21, 23, 25, 27, 37, 43, 51, 61;
Ross Sanderson page 9; Steve Tanner page 31;
cameraman Paul Ward page 59

Edited by Susan Daniel-McElroy, Sara Hughes and Kerry Rice
Design by Andrew Smith
Repro and print by Eden Print

Front cover image
Sax Impey, *Event 9* 2005, Mixed media on wood,
204 x 204 cm © the Artist

Measurements of artworks given in centimeters, height and width

St IVES
TATE